Pictures can and do make a difference. Strong images of historical events do have an impact on society. They can help with change.

—Charles Moore, photojournalist

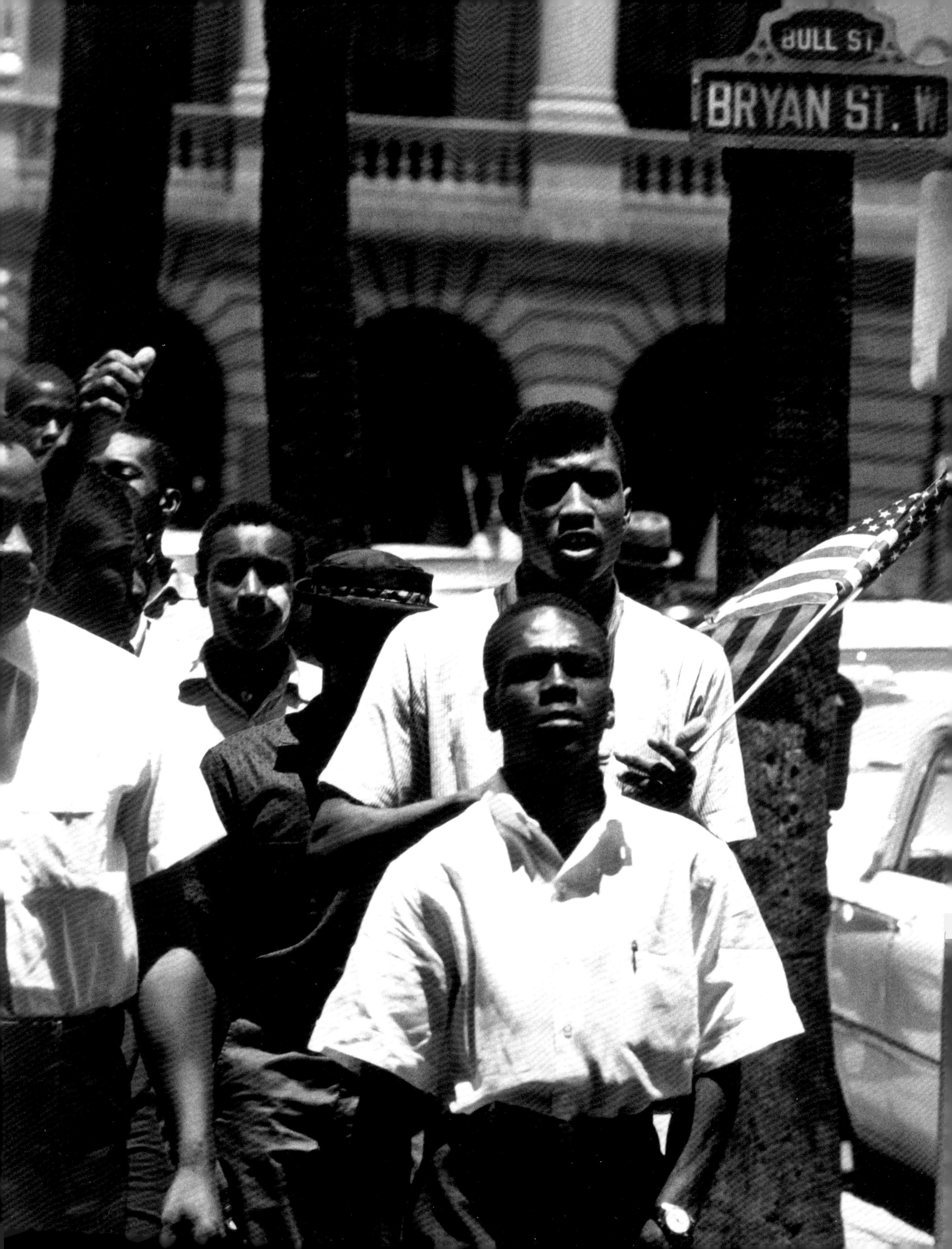

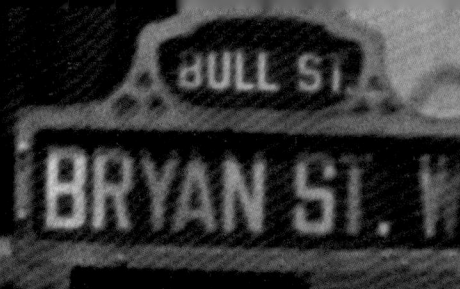

Freedom's March

Photographs of the Civil Rights Movement
in Savannah by Frederick C. Baldwin

Freedom's March

Photographs of the Civil Rights Movement
in Savannah by Frederick C. Baldwin

September 24, 2008 – January 11, 2009
Jepson Center for the Arts
This exhibition is organized by the Telfair Museum of Art
Savannah, Georgia
Funding provided through a *Museum and Community Connections* grant
from MetLife Foundation and by the City of Savannah

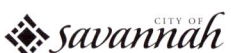

©2008 Telfair Books
All rights reserved. This book may not be reproduced in whole or in part,
in any form, without permission from the publisher.

ISBN-10: 0-933075-08-1
ISBN-13: 978-0-933075-08-5
Library of Congress Catalogue Control Number: 2008907146

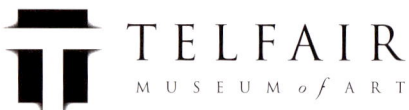

Published by Telfair Books
Distributed by the University of Georgia Press
www.ugapress.uga.edu

Printed in Canada

COVER FRONT:
Singing Freedom Songs
(See Plate 27)

COVER BACK:
Freedom or Death
(See Plate 21)

TITLE PAGE:
*Benjamin Van Clark Leading
a March, Bull Street*
(See Plate 20)

Contents

Director's Foreword	2
Seeds of the Modern Civil Rights Movement Were Planted in Georgia Michael Thurmond	4
Reflections on Freedom's March Otis S. Johnson	6
The Struggle for Civil Rights in Savannah Martha Keber	9
Freedom's March in Savannah: Documentary Photography, Social Reform, and Frederick C. Baldwin Holly Koons McCullough	17
Image Plates and Community Recollections	22
Prologue: Racism and Segregation	24
Voter Registration	28
The Chatham County Crusade for Voters: Leadership, Organization, Strategy	45
Sit-Ins, Day Marches, Night Marches	54
Arrests and Jail	67
Broad-based Support of the Civil Rights Movement	70
The Countermovement	76
Keys to Success	78
Epilogue: Dr. King	86
Image Plate Checklist	104

Director's Foreword

Steven High

Director,
Telfair Museum of Art

Forty-five years ago, the photographer and journalist Frederick Baldwin returned to Savannah, a city he had lived in and visited intermittently throughout his life. An emerging photojournalist and naturalist, Baldwin arrived in Savannah at a critical moment in our city's history. The summer of 1963 and early 1964 marked the culmination of demonstrations, marches, and advocacy by Savannah's African American community that resulted in the relatively peaceful desegregation of the city. During his stay in Savannah, Baldwin followed the advocacy efforts of key individuals in the African American community. His images are remarkable chronicles – notable not for sensationalist imagery of violence or protest, but for recording the mobilization and individual leadership of the time. His photographs document the intensive grassroots organization efforts to increase African American voter registration, demonstrations, and prayer services in the city's squares, and culminate in a powerful series chronicling Martin Luther King's address at Municipal Auditorium in 1964. With a photojournalist's eye, Baldwin captured images that revealed the energy and anxiety, the celebration and anticipation of this significant moment in the history of our city.

In 1983, twenty years after the events of late summer and fall 1963, the Telfair organized an exhibition and publication, both entitled, "...*We ain't what we used to be*.," which presented these images for the first time. The museum, then under the curatorial direction of Feay Shellman, exhibited the photographs accompanied by oral histories of the people who participated in these events. The accompanying catalogue combined the oral histories and photographs and became an important record of the civil rights era in Savannah.

With the catalogue long out of print, in 2008 the Telfair Museum began a new project to reinstall the photographs and to re-publish the images and oral histories. Under the curatorial guidance of Holly Koons McCullough, chief curator of fine arts and exhibitions at the Telfair, and the educational vision of Harry DeLorme, senior curator of education, we are once again proud to present the 1963-64 civil rights work of Frederick Baldwin to our community. Accompanying the exhibition *Freedom's March: Photographs of the Civil Rights Movement in Savannah by Frederick C. Baldwin* is a new version of the catalogue that reconfigures the original publication and supplements it with additional historical material and writings. In addition, the Telfair has been in partnership with a number of leading educational and cultural organizations within Savannah in order to build a comprehensive community-based selection of educational programs to accompany the exhibition.

Frederick Baldwin has been a great partner in this project, allowing us to exhibit his photographs once again and providing additional material about his time in Savannah. Now president of FotoFest in Houston, Texas, Baldwin continues to be a strong advocate of social activism and education through photography. Thanks also to Feay Shellman Coleman, former Telfair curator and collector/transcriber of the oral histories excerpted in the first catalogue, for the vision and commitment to present the first exhibition in 1983 and for allowing us to reprint some of her original material in this publication.

We are proud to feature new contributions in this publication by Savannah Mayor Otis Johnson and by Michael L. Thurmond, Georgia's Commissioner of Labor and author of *Freedom: Georgia's Antislavery Heritage, 1733-1865*. Mayor Johnson relates personal and powerful remembrances of the time and reinforces our need to continue the work toward true integration, while Michael Thurmond writes about the genesis of the civil rights movement in Georgia's history. We also thank Martha Keber for allowing us to use her adapted text from *Low Land and the High Road: Life and Community in Hudson Hill, West Savannah, and Woodville Neighborhoods*, published in 2008 by the City of Savannah's Department of Cultural Affairs, and Michelle Hunter, at the Department of Cultural Affairs, for negotiating the use of Martha Keber's text and for the rights to reproduce several accompanying images.

The Telfair thanks all of those individuals and organizations who have partnered with us on the educational programs surrounding *Freedom's March*. Participating in our community review panel were Ralph Mark Gilbert Civil Rights Museum, Diaspora Marketplace, Beach Institute, Chatham-Savannah Citizen Advocacy, Sentient Bean, Telfair's Friends of African American Arts, Indigo Sky Gallery, Georgia Historical Society, Senior Citizens Inc., Savannah State University, Armstrong Atlantic State University, 100 Black Men of Savannah, Jewish Education Alliance, Interdenominational Ministerial Alliance, City of Savannah Department of Cultural Affairs, and Trinity Methodist Church. In addition, Burton Sauls at CityTrex developed a web-based mp3 audio component for the oral history narratives.

At the Telfair, thanks go to the dedicated curatorial and education staffs including interns Cheryl Bartley and Josephine Warshauer for their work on the oral histories; Johnna Gluth, Beth Moore, and Jessica Mumford for coordination, research, and registration support; Vaughnette Goode-Walker for her organization of the community review panel; and Sara Ward, Torrey Stifel, and Marta McWhorter for managing educational programming during the exhibition. Alicia Griffiths designed the catalogue and Kate Hoernle edited all of the original text for this fine publication.

We are indebted to MetLife Foundation for its generous support of the exhibition, publication, and educational programs for *Freedom's March*. Thanks to MetLife's early and significant sponsorship, this project will reach the wide and diverse audience we envisioned. Finally, my appreciation goes out to the Telfair Museum of Art's board of trustees, whose vision and financial support enable us to present this exhibition to our community. ■

Seeds of the Modern Civil Rights Movement Were Planted in Georgia

Michael Thurmond

Commissioner of Labor, State of Georgia

Georgia has been a touchstone of controversy and a beacon of hope in the African American struggle for equality not only during the modern civil rights era, but from its very founding. In 1733, General James Oglethorpe settled Georgia as an anti-slavery colony. But Oglethorpe's ruling would soon be overturned, and the legalization of slavery in 1750 paved the way for a century of struggle.

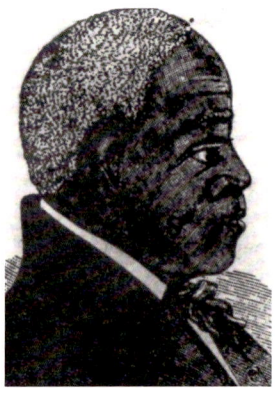

Throughout Georgia history, thousands of nameless, faceless black Georgians lived, fought, and died for freedom. The colony, and later the state, was located at the center of a politically and militarily unstable region. Georgia slaves, emboldened by a desire for freedom, shrewdly manipulated this international struggle for control of the southeastern section of North America to their advantage. They formed strategic and shifting alliances with the major contestants: England, Spain, the United States, and Native Americans. In addition, several thousand fugitive Georgia slaves escaped to freedom on the lesser-known "Underground Railroad" that ran south— across the international border between Georgia and Spanish-controlled Florida.

IMAGES (CLOCKWISE)

Savannah's First African Baptist Church (c.1790), one of the world's oldest black churches

Reverend Andrew Bryan, a free black Georgian and pastor of the First African Baptist Church

Reverend George Liele, the first black man ordained to preach in North America

Courtesy of First African Baptist Church

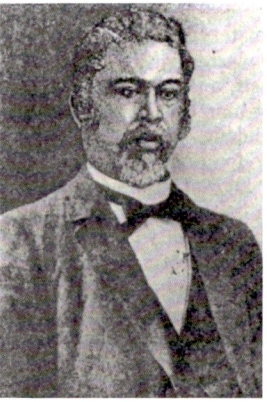

Yet escape and armed struggle were not the only strategies utilized by black slaves to secure the precious commodity called freedom. So-called "loyal" slaves shed blood by the sides of white slave owners when freedom was offered as compensation for military service. Following the completion of their masters' work, some enterprising blacks were allowed to "hire themselves out," eventually earning enough money to purchase freedom for themselves and their loved ones. The magnitude and scope of these events are unique to Georgia history.

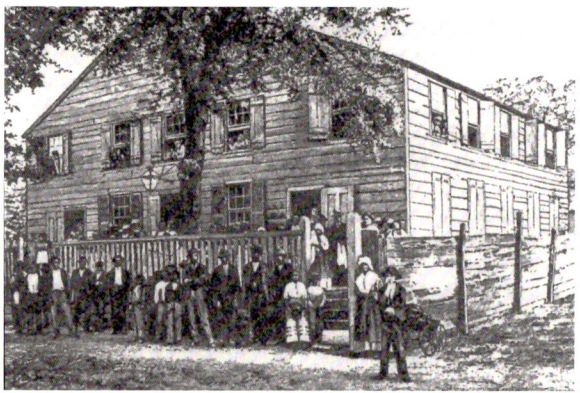

Freedom-loving black Georgians broke the shackles of bondage through escape, armed struggle, organized resistance, and individual acts of defiance. Fugitive Georgia slaves preserved their freedom by helping the Spanish repel British invaders from Florida during the colonial era. The Revolutionary War provided black Georgians with the opportunity to earn their freedom by serving the British as soldiers, spies, guides, orderlies, and laborers. Following the occupation of Cumberland Island by the British during the War of 1812, hundreds of coastal Georgia slaves answered their call to arms and emancipation. And early in the nineteenth century, fugitive Georgia slaves formed a powerful bi-racial coalition with Seminole Indians, stymieing American expansion into Florida for three decades.

Decades before Dr. Martin Luther King Jr., a native Georgian, gained international prominence as the leader of the modern civil rights movement, generations of enslaved blacks waged a historic struggle to abolish slavery in Georgia. In many ways, Georgia's past became America's prologue. The 1960s civil rights movement was not an isolated historical event, but the continuation of a protracted struggle that spanned more than twelve generations. More significantly, the origins of black America's struggle for freedom and justice are firmly rooted in Georgia's red clay soil. ■

Reflections on Freedom's March

Otis S. Johnson, PhD
Mayor, City of Savannah

"If there is no struggle there is no progress."

—Frederick Douglass, 1849

My life in Savannah is a reflection of the title of the Telfair Museum of Art's 2008 Baldwin exhibit, *Freedom's March*. I was born in 1942 during the heyday of the Jim Crow era of racial segregation in the South. I grew up in a segregated neighborhood on the eastside of Savannah where Blackshear Homes is today. I now live in a mixed race neighborhood, Baldwin Park. The only whites in my old neighborhood were shop owners who lived over or in back of their businesses. They were European immigrants who were getting their start as Americans. Ironically, housing patterns in Savannah allowed both blacks and whites–especially Irish, Jews, Greeks, Italians, and other second wave immigrants–to live in predominantly black neighborhoods. Many of these whites built their economic bases by trading with black people. There was an unwritten, but well understood, code that defined the rules of social engagement in these neighborhoods, especially between black males and white females. The older you became, the more social distance was expected. Over the years, the white families grew prosperous and began to move to the emerging all-white suburbs with the help of federal housing policy. Fellwood Homes and Yamacraw Village were low-income public housing complexes built for blacks with federal money. Federal policy would bring urban renewal into traditional black neighborhoods and result in what is commonly referred to as "Negro removal." The prosperous black business district along West Broad Street, now Martin Luther King Boulevard, was destroyed by the construction of the Kayton and Frazier public housing complexes and the I-16 highway overpass that segregated inhabitants of the mostly white Historic Landmark District from those of the predominately black residential area to the south of the overpass. Federal policies effectively ended the traditional desegregated housing pattern in Savannah. The Old Fort district on the eastside was destroyed, and a segregated public housing complex was built (Fred Wessels, white, and Robert High, black). The Old Fort was an area where many of the Irish lived and worked with blacks. Further east, Garden Homes was built for whites. Garden Homes has been replaced by Ashley Midtown, a mixed-income development. It may have a population that has mixed income, but it is at least 90% black. Gentrification is the twenty-first-century threat to desegregated housing in Savannah.

My grandfather, my brother, and I went to the Municipal Auditorium in January 1964 to hear Dr. Martin Luther King Jr. give a speech, an event well documented in Baldwin's photos. This was one of the proudest moments of my young life, to see in person our "Moses." I have the greatest respect for Dr. King, but he was incorrect when he said that Savannah was the most integrated city south of the Mason-Dixon Line.[1] Dr. King would certainly not be able to say that about Savannah in 2008. He was probably referring to the fact that the black and white leadership had negotiated a pact to end the segregation of lunch counters, theaters, and other public accommodations in the downtown area. To Savannah's credit, this pact was signed a year before the 1964 Civil Rights Act was passed by Congress and signed into law by President Lyndon Baines Johnson. I know of several restaurants and other businesses that closed rather than desegregate. You can mandate desegregation, but you cannot mandate integration. Integration must be an act of the heart, not a legal mandate. This principle speaks to the desegregation of schools and houses of worship.

Eleven o'clock on Sunday morning is still the most segregated hour in Savannah. There has been some desegregation of churches, but most people worship with folk who look just like them. That is the way it has been since the time of slavery. There are several small interfaith groups that are waging a gallant struggle to be interracial and to encourage respect for other forms of diversity in our community. Most social gatherings in Savannah are still segregated. There is tokenism at certain functions to avoid criticism, but social functions are as racially segregated as religious functions. Social functions are where race and class intersect. Birds of a feather are still flocking together.

I remember being a student at the racially segregated Paulsen Street Elementary School when the U.S. Supreme Court ruled in 1954 that the apartheid system of segregated schools violated the constitutional rights of black children. I graduated six years later in 1960 from a still segregated Alfred Eli Beach High School after having studied for twelve years using secondhand books from white schools. The first desegregated class I attended would be in 1963 when I became the first black to attend Armstrong State College, now Armstrong Atlantic State University. Local public schools would not desegregate until 1963, after a federal court battle with the Stell vs. The Board of Education case. Nineteen black students would attend two high schools (Groves and Savannah High) during the 1963-64 school year. It was not until a federal judge mandated busing in 1971 that the local school district moved beyond token desegregation efforts. This led to a massive exodus of white students from the public schools. The school district in 1971 reflected the approximately 60 percent white, 40 percent black population of Chatham County, then and now. The present school population is about 67 percent black. There are several schools that are 90 percent black because of the way attendance zones are drawn and special program policies. Racial disparities in academic outcomes are disturbing. Black males, especially, are having a difficult time experiencing success in the public schools. They have the highest suspension rate and the lowest graduation rate. Things ain't what they used to be, but they sure ain't what they ought to be.

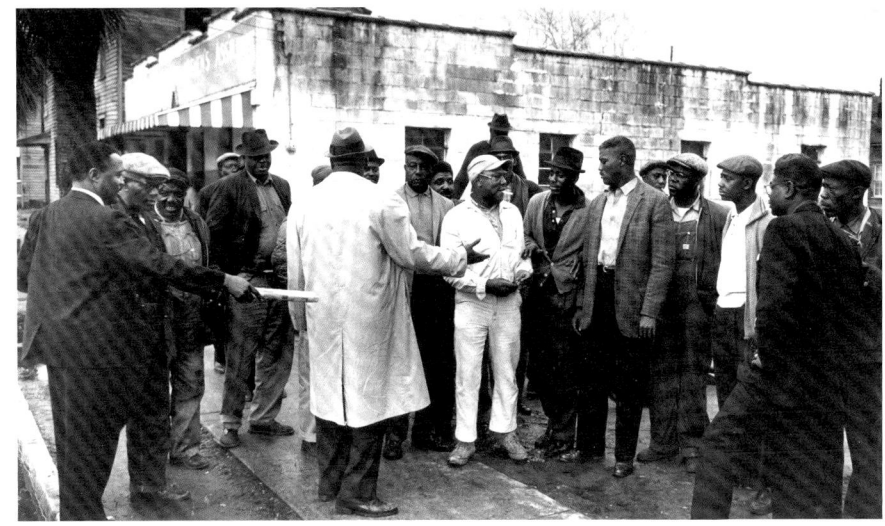

Frederick C. Baldwin
(American, b. 1929)
"Big Lester" Among the Longshoremen II, Longshoremen's Hall, 1964
9 x 13⅞ inches
Long-term loan from the artist to the Telfair Museum of Art

There were no local black elected officials when I graduated from high school in 1960. I am now the second black to be Mayor of Savannah. In 1967, attorney Bobby Hill became the first black elected to public office in Chatham County since Reconstruction. Chatham County is now represented by a black state senator and three black state representatives. Presently, the majority of Savannah's City Council is black. There are three county commissioners, three school board members, and several elected judges. Blacks serve on all the major appointed commissions and boards. In 1960, I had no dream of going to college or becoming Mayor of the City of Savannah. I joined the U.S. Naval Reserve during my junior year of high school and went on active duty for two years after graduation. But I had caught the civil rights fever and was destined to a life of advocacy. Two of my homeroom classmates, Carolyn Quilloin and Joan Tyson, were among those NAACP Youth Council members arrested on March 16, 1960, for sitting-in at the Levy Department Store Azalea Room restaurant. The first and only time I was suspended from school was when a group of students left Beach High School to attend the police court hearing for our friends. I was away in the Navy during the historic downtown boycott, but was back in time for the 1963 demonstrations documented by Baldwin. We sure ain't where we used to be in the political arena.

The civil rights movement was beginning to shift its focus from school desegregation, public accommodations, and voting rights to economic justice in the late 1960s. I believe this shift in emphasis and opposition to the Viet Nam War are what finally caused the assassination of Dr. King. He was planning a "Poor People's Movement" to bring together groups suffering from poverty and economic disadvantage and demand an end to the policies and practices responsible for creating and sustaining these conditions in the United States. In other words, Dr. King had moved beyond the fight for racial desegregation to the struggle for social integration. He was beginning the struggle to bring disadvantaged groups into the mainstream of American society to provide them access to the opportunities, rights, and services available to the members of the general population. Currently, 22 percent (27,000) of the citizens of Savannah live in persistent poverty. Eighty percent of these people are black. This is about the same situation that existed in 1967 when I started my first professional job with the Economic Opportunity Authority, the Great Society anti-poverty program in Savannah. Economic integration is the real unfinished work of Dr. King that must be carried on by those of us who are still alive. The current Step Up Poverty Reduction Initiative has the potential of moving more Savannahians into the economic mainstream. Step Up has brought together more than eighty public and private organizations to fight persistent poverty in Savannah. We ain't where we should be, but we are moving in the right direction.

Space will not allow me to go on with my reflections. One day, I will finish my memoir about growing up in Savannah. *Freedom's March* serves as a reminder that the struggle in Savannah and all across America was waged by, and must be continued by, courageous men and women, boys and girls, who answer the call to hold our country to its highest ideals as expressed in the Declaration of Independence, the Constitution, and the Bill of Rights. We must remain committed to creating that more perfect Union. I promise to remain strong and stay in the struggle. What about you? ∎

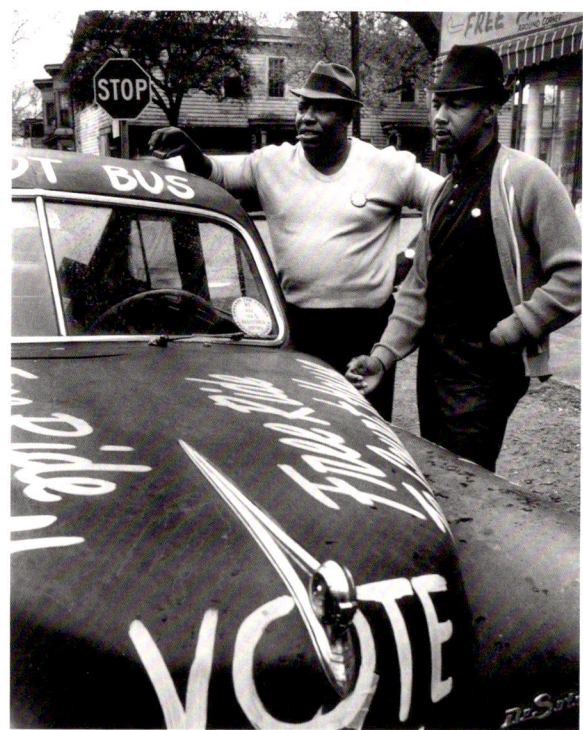

Frederick C. Baldwin (American, b. 1929)
The Ballot Bus II, 1964
13 1/16 x 9 inches
Long-term loan from the artist
to the Telfair Museum of Art

---

[1] Telfair Academy of Arts and Sciences, *"…We ain't what we used to be." Photographs by Frederick C. Baldwin* (Savannah: Telfair Academy of Arts and Sciences, 1983), 68.

The Struggle for Civil Rights in Savannah

Martha Keber
Author and Historian

Early Activism

African Americans in Savannah have fought racial discrimination since Jim Crow laws imposed segregation in the late nineteenth century. Often it was the small acts of daily living that became the battleground for equality. In 1906, for example, the Savannah City Council passed an ordinance requiring separate cars for black and white passengers on streetcars. For more than thirty years, streetcars had been integrated, thanks to an 1870 Georgia law banning racial discrimination in public transport. Black residents boycotted the streetcars in 1907, walking or hiring a hack in defiance of the Jim Crow ordinance. Although the boycott was total and lasted over eighteen months, it failed to stop the segregation policy.[1]

The call for struggle against racism also came in the blazing headlines of the *Chicago Defender*, the most influential African American newspaper in the United States in the early twentieth century. Robert Abbott, who grew up in Woodville, three miles west of the Savannah city limits, founded the *Defender* in 1905 and served as editor and publisher until his death in 1940. Abbott's newspaper became the voice of social justice for many Southern blacks. In 1916, the *Defender* urged African Americans to leave the lynchings and meager wages of the Jim Crow South to come north for a better life.[2] Acting on Abbott's call for a "great migration" of Southern black workers, 2,500 black Savannahians boarded two north-bound labor trains during the summer of 1916. Even when the labor trains stopped running, workers left Savannah at a rate of a hundred per week in 1917, rather than accept the indignities of the segregated South.[3]

The Rise of the NAACP

In 1917, a Savannah branch of the National Association for the Advancement of Colored People (NAACP) was established. Annual dues of one dollar were set in hopes of attracting a wide membership from the African American community.[4] Unfortunately, membership dropped off so sharply during the Depression that the national office revoked the Savannah charter in 1939. It was the arrival of a new pastor at First African Baptist Church in that year that sparked the revival of the NAACP in Savannah.

Dr. Ralph Mark Gilbert was a natural leader. A superb speaker, he delivered sermons and speeches that profoundly moved his audiences. His charisma drew followers to him, and he understood the necessity of excellent organization to achieve his goals.[5] A native of Savannah, Dr. Gilbert returned home after a pastorate in Detroit, determined to revive the NAACP in his hometown. He called for a mass meeting in February 1942, inviting "all interested citizens" to show their support for a reinvigorated NAACP presence in Savannah.[6] Dr. Gilbert saw the potential of the mass meeting to rally public opinion, and that technique became an important weapon in the civil rights movement in Savannah in the 1960s. The national office of the NAACP created a new branch with the urging of Dr. Gilbert and other concerned Savannahians. To no one's surprise, Dr. Gilbert took charge of the new branch as president, a position he held from 1942 to 1950. Leaders of other NAACP branches across Georgia recognized his talents, and Dr. Gilbert was elected president of the statewide organization in 1942.[7]

This text was adapted by author Martha Keber from its original form in the book *Low Land and the High Road: Life and Community in Hudson Hill, West Savannah, and Woodville Neighborhoods* (copyright 2008) with generous permission from its publisher, the City of Savannah's Department of Cultural Affairs.

Much of the energy of the NAACP in the 1940s focused on voter registration. Dr. Gilbert was tireless in his efforts to give black Savannahians political power through the vote. By 1948, 20,000 black men and women had registered in the city, and block voting assured that their voices would be heard.[8]

Dr. Gilbert also courted the younger generation. The Youth Council was a means of bringing teenagers into the movement. Their energy was a resource of great value to the NAACP, and, in time, young people who worked in registration drives would become voters themselves. High school chapters and theater parties sponsored by the Youth Council attracted students. In 1948, for example, *The Herald* advertised a special showing of *The Voice of the Turtle* for students at the Dunbar Theater. The invitation to join the fun on West Broad Street also included another call: "Register to vote and join the NAACP at once."[9] Dr. Gilbert's embrace of youth participation showed his insight into one of the most dynamic parts of a mass movement. By 1943, the Youth Council in Savannah was the largest of any NAACP branch in the country.[10]

Building such a movement and arming it with the vote gave the NAACP the muscle to press for change. The integration of the Savannah Police Department was one important issue which required attention. Dr. Gilbert pushed Mayor John Kennedy to hire black policemen, and on May 1, 1947, nine African American men joined the Savannah Police Department. The "Original Nine" who broke the color line at the police department still found discrimination existing on the job. African American officers patrolled only black neighborhoods and arrested only black suspects. Racial considerations still restricted their assignments and authority to West Broad Street. They had no contact with white policemen or the police barracks on Habersham Street. Instead, they had separate barracks on West Waldburg Street.[11] Even as more black officers joined the force, integration was still only "skin deep" at the Savannah Police Department.

In 1948, a new county ordinance invalidated the roll of registered voters, forcing black citizens to take literacy tests intended to deny them voting rights. With the 1948 Dixiecrat campaign of Strom Thurmond, segregation intensified across Georgia and the South. Ralph Mark Gilbert, in failing health, resigned from his post as president of the Savannah branch of the NAACP in 1950, and Westley Wallace Law succeeded him.[12]

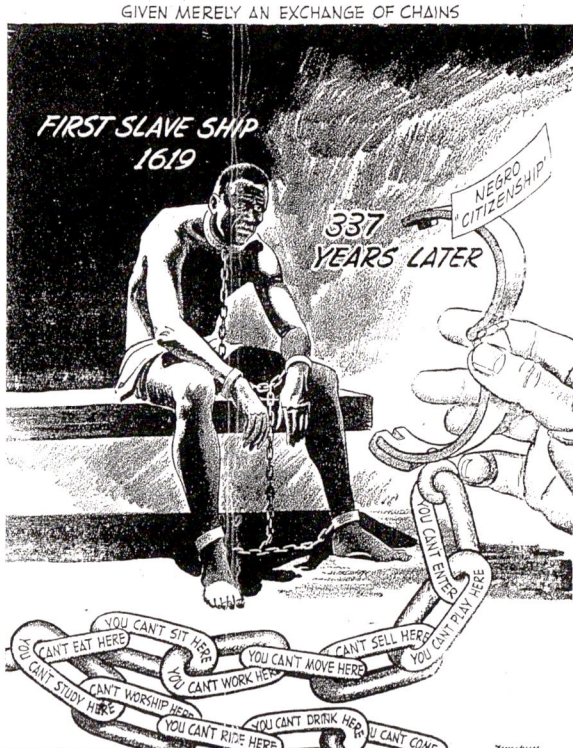

Fig. 1 Editorial Cartoon, *The Herald*, 3 May 1956
Courtesy of *The Herald*

W.W. Law joined the Youth Council as a high school student and was elected its president in 1946 while attending Savannah State College. Thanks to Dr. Gilbert, the movement that W.W. Law inherited was active and organized, despite the recent setbacks. He added his own brand of charisma that energized the Savannah branch.

Like his mentor, Law believed in the Youth Council. "Membership [in] the Youth Council," he said, "became a badge of honor and practically every student in the school joined."[13] Slogans made it clear that young people were essential to the movement: "We need the youth, the youth need us. Join us!" And for fifty cents in annual dues, young people from twelve to sixteen years old could sign up; older youth between seventeen and twenty-five paid one dollar in dues. In 1961, the Savannah branch proudly counted 650 members in the Youth Council.[14]

The NAACP's message created not only the hope for change but an impatience to move forward. The restrictions of a segregated society weighed heavily on all, but there was a growing expectation, especially among the youth, that the time for action had come. A college student and graduate of Tompkins High School, James German spoke for his generation: "It was really rough, because that was all you knew, segregation and all that, when you were coming up. You don't go here, you don't do that. So, you don't do it! Until somebody broke out and said, 'this is wrong.'"[15]

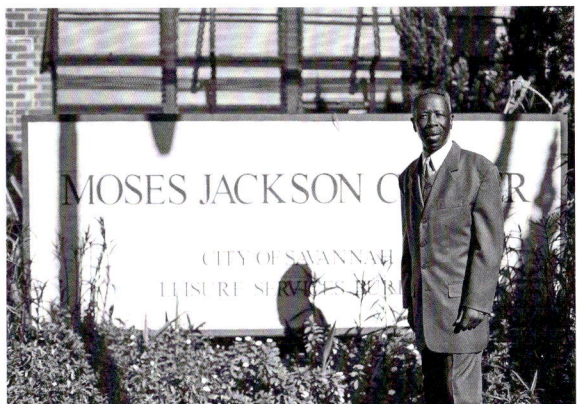

Fig. 2 The grandson of West Savannah community leader Moses Jackson, James Jackson founded his own activist group in 1960 and participated in the sit-ins. He was arrested at Livingston's Drug Store on March 19, 1960.

Courtesy of Colin Douglas Gray

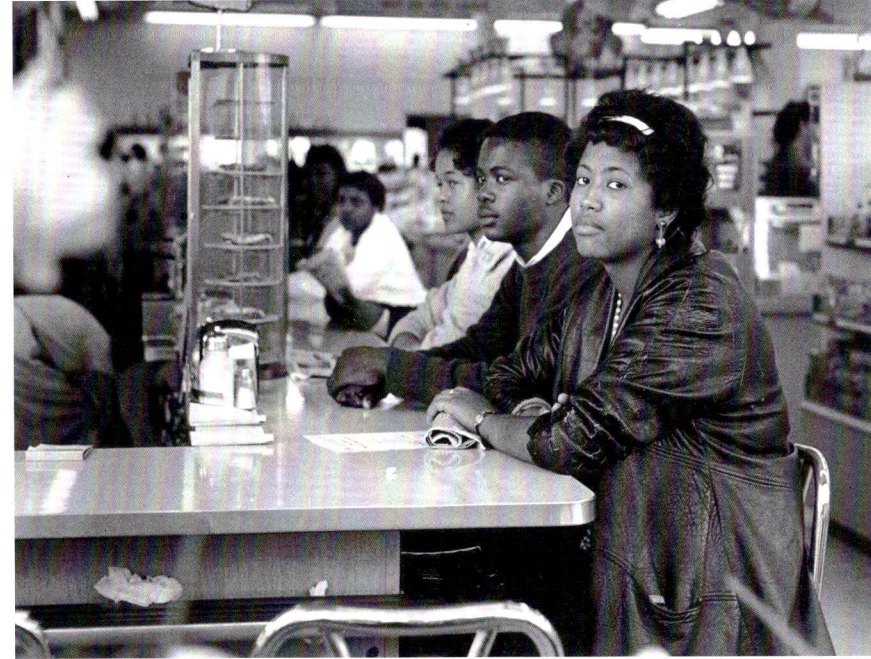

Fig. 3 Sit-ins at Broughton Street lunch counters continued for more than a year. On March 23, 1961, students occupied lunch counter seats at McCrory's in silent protest.

Courtesy of the *Savannah Morning News*

Sit-Ins

Student sit-ins in Greensboro, North Carolina, in February 1960 inspired the Savannah Youth Council to take the initiative. On March 16, groups of students walked into Broughton Street stores and asked for service at the lunch counters. Police turned away the students at Silver's 5¢ and 10¢ store, but the young people were undeterred. The students made their way down the street, stopping at McCrory's, Kress, Livingston's Drug Store, Woolworth's, W.T. Grant's, and Walgreen's. Lunch counters closed as soon as they sat down. Finally, police arrested Carolyn Quilloin, Ernest Robinson, and Joan Tyson for trespassing when they sat down at the lunch counter of the Azalea Room in Levy's Department Store and requested service. Jailed overnight, the students stated that their actions were their own, not the result of prodding by the NAACP.[16]

The significance of that first sit-in may not have registered in Savannah's white community at first. The *Savannah Morning News* on the following day focused on Saint Patrick's Day festivities, and the report of the sit-ins and arrests was buried in the interior of the paper. But the news electrified the African American community and spurred the NAACP Executive Board to take up the students' crusade. Curtis Cooper, a member of the Executive Board, said of the students, "I guess it was just a case of a little child leading us. . . .'Cause when they did it, [and] they got in jail, we began to respond."[17]

The NAACP trained youth in nonviolence. Whatever the provocation might be—name-calling, spitting, shoves, or punches—the young people turned the other cheek. "We had to make sure we didn't send out any hotheads," said Cooper, or "you just defeat the purpose."[18] Benjamin West, a graduate of Tompkins High School, was known as a man who could take the abuse. At one sit-in at Kress, he was unmoved when whites spat on him. Even when someone slugged him and broke his jaw, he refused to retaliate.[19]

Despite fierce opposition, the sit-ins continued. Woolworth's, McCrory's, Kress, and Levy's were targeted repeatedly. The protesters were so familiar to employees that they closed down the lunch counters before the young people said a word. At times, there were twelve or fifteen protesters sitting at a closed lunch counter so that no one else could sit there either.[20]

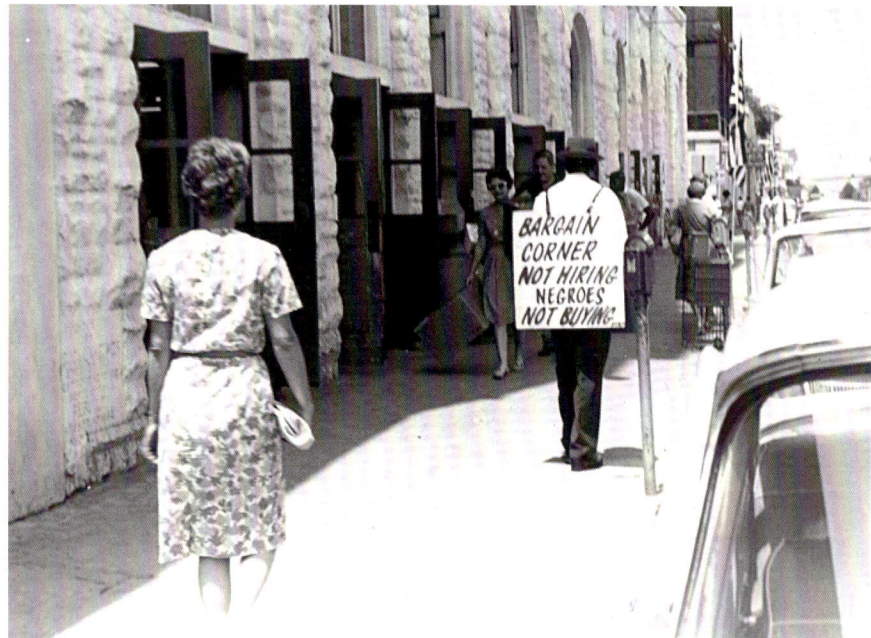

The Broughton Street Boycott

It quickly became apparent that the sit-ins alone were not going to change the segregation policies of merchants. The NAACP leadership realized that the time had arrived to press for change on a much wider scale. African Americans wanted more than service at lunch counters. They wanted jobs in retail; as customers, they wanted to be addressed respectfully as "Mr." and "Mrs." instead of by first names; they wanted to use rest rooms, water fountains, and dressing rooms in stores; and they wanted the same access to restaurants, movie theaters, and hotels as whites.[21] The Broughton Street Boycott began in late March 1960. Black shoppers cut up their charge cards and vowed to stay away. Even the tradition of purchasing new clothes for Easter was forgotten that spring by many black families.

The NAACP's Boycott Committee organized picketing. Legally, only two picketers carrying placards were permitted at a time, but "silent picketing" was a way around the law. People wearing single black ribbons walked up and down the street. They carried no signs or posters, but they helped to enforce the boycott.[22] One target was the Bargain Corner on Bay Street, a grocery and general store where many black families shopped.

The boycott that began in the spring lasted month after month, and the sit-ins continued as well. In the summer, there was a "wade-in" at Tybee to protest segregated Savannah Beach. A "kneel-in" followed in October as students tried to attend Sunday services at white churches. There were also "ride-ins" on the buses and "stand-ins" at the movie theaters.[23]

The boycott took its toll on Broughton Street merchants. A few went out of business, but all suffered significant losses in revenue. At the negotiating table, the NAACP sat down with the merchants, as well as city and community leaders. A settlement gave African Americans desegregated lunch counters, courtesy titles, and free access to rest rooms, water fountains, and dressing rooms. The merchants promised more jobs. In October 1961, the boycott ended after eighteen months.[24]

Fig. 4 Curtis Cooper, who chaired the Boycott Committee for the NAACP, walked the picket line on Bay Street demanding jobs for African Americans at Bargain Corner.

Courtesy of Constance Cooper

Voter Registration

Voter registration had been a priority for the NAACP since the days of Dr. Ralph Mark Gilbert, and it continued in the 1950s even after obstacles such as literacy tests were designed to keep black citizens off the voting rolls. The registration drive intensified in the early 1960s under the leadership of Hosea Williams and the Chatham County Crusade for Voters (CCCV), the political wing of the NAACP. This campaign climaxed an effort that had been ongoing since the early 1950s and by 1962, over 17,000 black voters had registered, representing 57 percent of all the adult African Americans in the county.[25]

Many individuals contributed to this success. The young people recruited their own in the high schools. As soon as a student turned eighteen, she or he was encouraged to register immediately. "Big Lester" Hankerson drove the Ballot Bus and inevitably filled it with prospective voters. Student activist Benjamin Van Clark remembered him this way:

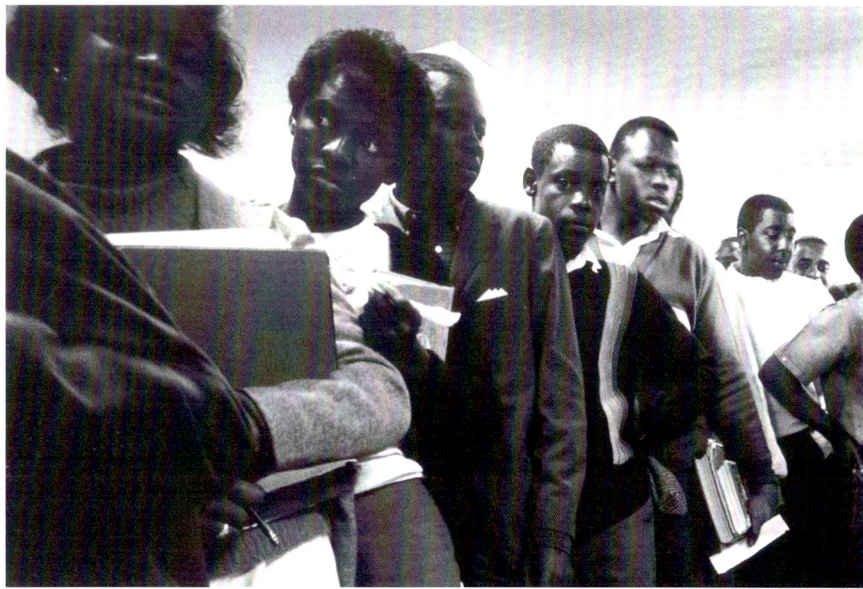

Fig. 5 These students came in a group to the courthouse to register.
Photograph by Frederick C. Baldwin (See Plate 5)
Long-term loan from the artist to the Telfair Museum of Art

> He loved the Ballot Bus. And guess what? I have seen him go on the corner and grab dudes—say, 'Looka here man!' He say, 'You register to vote?' 'No.' 'Come on—get in.' 'Lester, I can't go nowhere with you right now!' 'You GONNA GET IN HERE!' Now that's his. You don't ever take that from him 'cause that's his![26]

A rough-talking, hard-living bully of a man, "Big Lester" converted to nonviolence but he never lost his powers of persuasion. He worked on his fellow longshoremen at the union hall of Local 1414 and convinced many members of the International Longshoremen's Association to register.

The CCCV and the Marches

Gradually, a difference in tactics emerged between W.W. Law and his second-in-command, Hosea Williams. That difference was reflected in the strategies and tactics used by the NAACP and the CCCV. Mr. Law preferred to work through the courts and through negotiation, but Hosea Williams built a base in the CCCV among the young people and the poor by calling for direct action. The CCCV declared its independence from the parent organization in October 1962, although the two groups stood united to the outside world.[27]

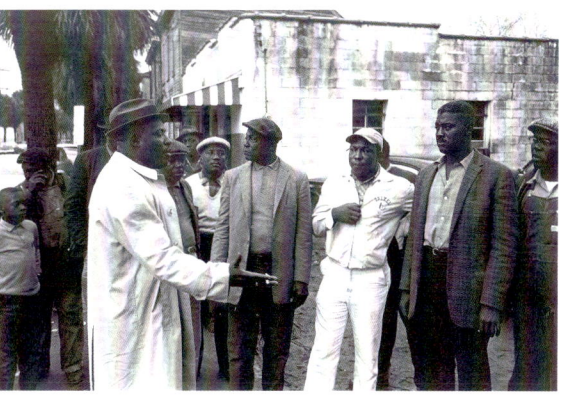

Fig. 6 "Big Lester" Hankerson, in overcoat, reaches out to longshoremen in 1964. He and "Trash" Brownlee, in white jacket, worked the union hall together.
Photograph by Frederick C. Baldwin (See Plate 6)
Long-term loan from the artist to the Telfair Museum of Art

The NAACP took a more aggressive stance to compete with Hosea Williams and his followers, but the long, hot summer of 1963 belonged to the CCCV.[28] When the movie theaters withdrew their promise to integrate in June, protesters demanded that segregation must end, not just in theaters but everywhere in Savannah. The tactic used by the CCCV was to overload the court system and the jails with arrested marchers and protesters.

CCCV members Sage Brown and George Shinhoster, Tompkins students who would help integrate Groves High School in the fall of 1963, spent the summer in and out of jail cells as regular marchers. "We knew if you marched, you were going to jail," remembered George Shinhoster. "It was like a badge of honor." Part of the attraction of the CCCV was its call for action. "It was not adults," said Sage Brown. "It was young people. It was a street movement, and it gave us a chance to be involved."[29]

It was the night marches that had the greatest potential for violence. As many as 3,000 people marched in an evening demonstration, protesting the court orders that barred them from disrupting business for restaurant owners or movie theaters. Some of the NAACP leaders feared that troublemakers might use the marches as a cover for criminal activity or that the crowds might get out of control.[30] James German, who joined some of the night marches, remembered the crowd preparing for a march at the Flamingo night club on Gwinnett Street when the police arrived to arrest them. "I think we did get kind of violent that night. It wasn't no lick-spat, I think we turned the paddy wagon over and everybody escaped."[31] In another incident, Hosea Williams was arrested and stayed in jail for a month when his bond was set at the impossible sum of $30,000. "Big Lester" summed up the efforts of the CCCV: "We went to jail about a thousand. We kept the city and county jails full. We marched morning, noon, and night."[32]

The sobering example of the violence in Birmingham and a genuine effort on the part of black and white leaders to come to a settlement ended Savannah's long, hot summer. By the fall of 1963, restaurants, movie theaters, golf courses, libraries, and hotels opened their doors to all. Businesses welcomed blacks as customers and as employees. Even if the settlement was imperfectly implemented at times, Savannah had a policy of integration months before the passage of the Civil Rights Act of 1964.[33]

School Desegregation: A Case Study of Groves High School

The year 1963 proved to be a watershed year on several fronts. Not only was a policy of desegregation of public facilities put into effect, but the Savannah-Chatham County Public Schools began a long process of integrating its classrooms. The 1954 Supreme Court ruling Brown vs. Board of Education mandated equality in education for all races, effectively overturning the "separate but equal" standard used to segregate schools. The NAACP branch in Savannah twice petitioned the Board of Education to comply with the ruling in 1955 and 1959, but there was no movement towards integration. Finally, in January 1962, Rev. L. Scott Stell and thirty-five other African American parents filed suit on behalf of their children to force the integration of the Savannah-Chatham County Public Schools. In the summer of 1963, the Fifth Circuit Court of Appeals ordered integration of the twelfth grade to begin that fall.[34]

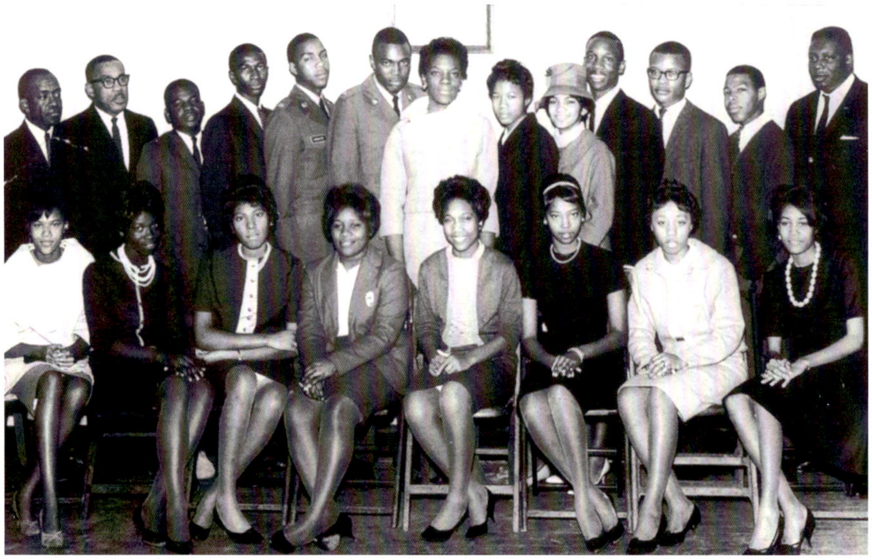

Nineteen high school students, all rising seniors in the summer of 1963, were chosen to integrate all-white Savannah High School and Groves High School. The experience of the seven African American students enrolled at Groves—Sage Brown, Martha Jean Coleman, Deloris Cooper, Flora Ann Goldwire, George Shinhoster, Sadie Mae Simmons, and Sara Townsend—is indicative of the difficulties all nineteen faced for the 1963-64 academic year.

In the weeks before school opened, the students learned to respond to taunts and attacks with nonviolence, but the sixteen- and seventeen-year-old students could hardly imagine what was in store. "I didn't want to go to Groves," said Sage Brown, a veteran of summer protest marches. "I expected it to be more trouble [than Savannah High]" because resentment against integration was believed to be stronger in Garden City. Flora Ann Goldwire, who lived in Garden City, agreed. "I knew it would be rough, but I didn't know how much."[35]

Fig. 7 The major figures in the 1963 desegregation efforts were, seated from left to right: Lillian Myers, Frankie Coleman, four unidentified, Sara Townsend, Geraldine Loadholt; standing, W.W. Law–president of Savannah Branch NAACP, L. Scott Stell–chairman of NAACP Education Committee, Robert Stephenson, Ulysses Bryant Jr., George Shinhoster, Sage Brown, Anistine Thompson, unidentified, Florence Russell, John Alexander, Robbie Robinson, Eddie Banner, and A.J. Scott.
Courtesy of the Ralph Mark Gilbert Civil Rights Museum

Under police escort, the Groves Seven began the school year under trying circumstances. They dodged food thrown at them in the lunchroom and spitballs in class; name-calling, racial slurs, and harassing phone calls added to the hostile environment. White students who reached out to their black classmates suffered retaliation. One teacher sent Sara Townsend to the principal's office every day because there was a pencil mark on her desk. There was some relief, she recalled, with the arrival of Principal J. Rife English, who joined the staff in mid-year. "He would come out and make sure we got off campus okay." At graduation, however, taunting continued; in May 1964, the seven received their diplomas to the sounds of booing.[36]

Memories of their senior year at Groves are still painful. "I had no friends at Groves other than those of color," said George Shinhoster. "There were a couple of white guys with a few kind words."[37] What the seven endured was, in Sage Brown's words, "a necessary price," but one that he would never ask of his own children. Flora Ann Goldwire summed up the determination of the group when she said, "I was definitely going to succeed because I wasn't going back the next year."[38]

Integration of the Savannah Fire Department

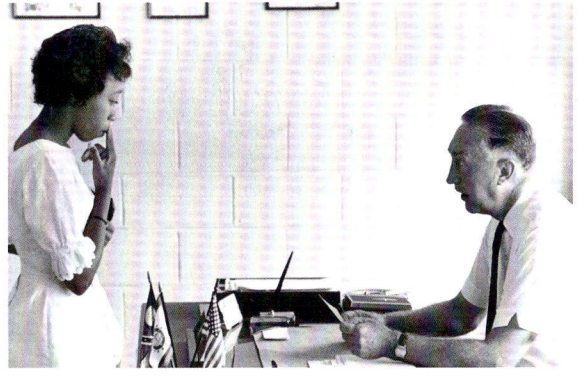

Fig. 8 Sara Townsend meets with Principal Donald Gray on a difficult first morning at Groves High School.
Savannah Morning News, 12 February 2006
Courtesy of the *Savannah Morning News*

The progress made towards integration was measured not just at the public schools but also at the Savannah Fire Department. Hiring black firemen seemed to be a logical step forward after the integration of the police department in 1947. But the issue was complicated by the fact that it was not just a question of black and white men fighting fires together; firemen lived together in tight quarters at the firehouse. In the 1950s, the African American community lobbied for an integrated fire department. At one point, there was a plan to construct a new firehouse where only black firemen worked, thus skirting the sensitive issue of sharing living space. Nothing came of the plan.[39] A 1959 editorial in *The Herald* railed against the political subterfuge that delayed any action. "Meanwhile," the editorial concluded, "there are no Negro firemen in the city, Negroes' homes still burn and lives are lost."[40] Ironically, it was slaves and free men of color who fought Savannah fires before the Civil War, and some black fire companies existed as late as the 1870s.[41]

Mayor Malcolm Maclean made an election pledge to hire black firemen, and he fulfilled that promise in 1963. Six men—Purdy Bowers, Cordell Heath, Lewis Oliver, Theodore Rivers, Warnell Robinson, and Porter Screen—joined the fire department on May 1 at Station #4 on East Lathrop Avenue. The choice of Station #4 in the predominantly black neighborhood of West Savannah was intended to isolate the firemen from white Savannahians in distress. The new recruits were further isolated with separate quarters. They had a separate bath, bedroom, kitchen, and television on one side of the firehouse. Gradually, the racial barriers eased as men from both sides of the station shared a meal or watched a game on television together.[42]

Conclusion

African Americans in Savannah had every right to take pride in the victories won at Station #4 and the lunch counters on Broughton Street. Those landmark events were the culmination of a struggle that had been ongoing for more than a century. But the quest for civil rights did not end at this point. After the Civil Rights Act of 1964 and other federal legislation, the struggle continued in court rooms and school buses and voting booths. Freedom's March of the 1960s was a defining period in Savannah's past, and its legacy of equality is the keystone for building a just society for all citizens. ∎

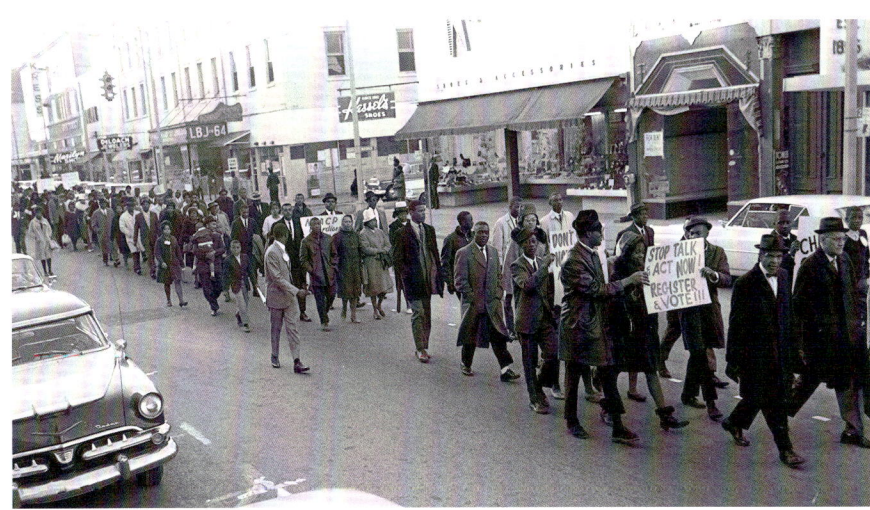

Fig. 9 Nearly 700 strong, marchers silently trekked to the Chatham County Courthouse in support of the Selma voter registration drive. *Savannah Morning News*, 21 March 1965.
Courtesy of the *Savannah Morning News*

[1] John W. Blassingame, "Before the Ghetto: The Making of the Black Community in Savannah, Georgia, 1865-1880," *Journal of Social History* (1973): 479-80; Robert E. Perdue, *The Negro in Savannah*, 1865-1900 (New York: Exposition Press, 1973), 33-34; Stephen G. N. Tuck, *Beyond Atlanta: The Struggle for Racial Equality in Georgia, 1940-1980* (Athens: University of Georgia Press, 2001), 46.

[2] Roi Ottley, *The Lonely Warrior* (Chicago: Henry Regnery, 1955), 159-61.

[3] *Savannah Tribune*, 19 August 1916, 1; Martin Terrell, "A Study of the *Chicago Defender's* 'Great Northern Drive' " (M.A. thesis, Ohio University, 1991), 73.

[4] Charles Lwanga Hoskins, *Out of Yamacraw and Beyond: Discovering Black Savannah* (Savannah: The Gullah Press, 2002), 15.

[5] Tuck, *Beyond Atlanta*, 44, 47.

[6] *Savannah Tribune*, 19 February 1942.

[7] Tuck, *Beyond Atlanta*, 48, 50.

[8] *Savannah Morning News*, 29 January 2005, 5A.

[9] *The Herald* (Savannah), 25 November 1948.

[10] Tuck, *Beyond Atlanta*, 48; Stephen Tuck, "A City Too Dignified to Hate: Civic Pride, Civil Rights, and Savannah in Comparative Perspective," *Georgia Historical Quarterly* 79 (Fall 1995): 557-58.

[11] Vertical Files, Afro-Americans—Civil Rights, Georgia Historical Society.

[12] Tuck, "Civic Pride, Civil Rights, and Savannah," 547, 558.

[13] Tuck, *Beyond Atlanta*, 48.

[14] Ibid., 133; *Herald*, 16 September 1954, 4 April 1959.

[15] Frederick C. Baldwin Interviews: James German, 4, Telfair Museum of Art.

[16] *Savannah Morning News*, 17 March 1960.

[17] Frederick C. Baldwin Interviews: Curtis Cooper, Tape 1, 1-2, Telfair Museum of Art.

[18] Ibid.

[19] Frederick C. Baldwin Interviews: James German, 2-3, Telfair Museum of Art.

[20] Frederick C. Baldwin Interviews: Curtis Cooper, Tape 1,15; James Middleton, 7, Telfair Museum of Art.

[21] Telfair Academy of Arts and Sciences, *"…We ain't what we used to be." Photographs by Frederick C. Baldwin* (Savannah: Telfair Academy of Arts and Sciences, 1983), 28.

[22] Frederick C. Baldwin Interviews: Curtis Cooper, Tape 2, 2-3, Telfair Museum of Art.

[23] *The Herald*, 3 September 1960, 8 October 1960; Tuck, "Civic Pride, Civil Rights, and Savannah," 546.

[24] Frederick C. Baldwin Interviews: Curtis Cooper, Tape 1, 3-5, Telfair Museum of Art; Tuck, *Beyond Atlanta*, 127, 134.

[25] Tuck, "Civic Pride, Civil Rights, and Savannah," 547.

[26] Telfair, *"…We ain't what we used to be."* 6.

[27] Tuck, "Civic Pride, Civil Rights, and Savannah," 547-48; Frederick C. Baldwin Interviews: Hosea Williams, 15–16, Telfair Museum of Art.

[28] Tuck, "Civic Pride, Civil Rights, and Savannah," 548; Frederick C. Baldwin Interviews: Sage Brown, 2, Telfair Museum of Art.

[29] *Savannah Morning News*, "Quest for Equality," 2.

[30] Ibid., 2–3.

[31] Frederick C. Baldwin Interviews: James German, 1, Telfair Museum of Art.

[32] Frederick C. Baldwin Interviews: Lester Hankerson, 2–3, Telfair Museum of Art.

[33] Frederick C. Baldwin Interviews: Curtis Cooper, Tape 1, 9-10, Telfair Museum of Art; Tuck, "Civic Pride, Civil Rights, and Savannah," 542.

[34] *The Herald*, 30 May 1959; *Savannah Morning News*, 16 May 2004, 4-6A.

[35] *Savannah Morning News*, 30 March 1997, 1E.

[36] Ibid., 2E; *Savannah Morning News*, 16 May 2004, 4A.

[37] *Savannah Morning News*, 30 March 1997, 2E.

[38] Ibid.; *Savannah Morning News*, 16 May 2004, 4A.

[39] *The Herald*, 4 April 1959, 4.

[40] Ibid.

[41] James E. Chase, "History of Savannah Council No. 1 of the Georgia State Council of American Firemen, also the Savannah Fire Department," (Savannah: the Morning News Printing Houses, 1898), 57061; John E. Maguire, "Historical Souvenir: Savannah Fire Department," (Savannah: Presses of M. S. & D.A. Byck, 1906), 16-17, 23. Both sources are available at the Georgia Room, Bull Street Branch of the Live Oak Public Libraries.

[42] Lewis Oliver, Oral History, Westside Documentation Project, Municipal Research Library.

Freedom's March in Savannah:
Documentary Photography, Social Reform, and Frederick C. Baldwin

Holly Koons McCullough
Chief Curator of Fine Arts & Exhibitions,
Telfair Museum of Art

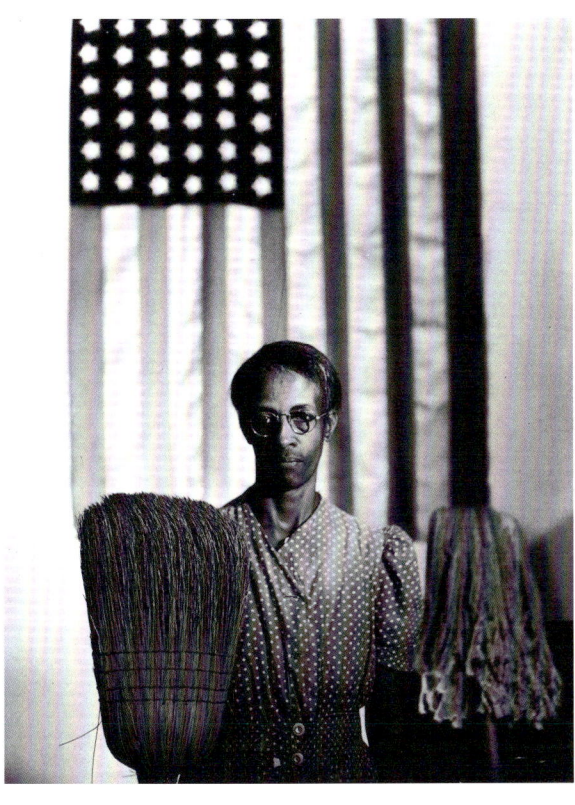

Fig. 1
Gordon Parks (American, 1912–2006)
American Gothic, Washington, D.C. (Ella Watson);
Gelatin silver print; Library of Congress,
Prints and Photographs Division; FSA-OWI Collection.

In 1963, Frederick Baldwin (b. 1929) returned to Savannah after several years in Europe to find the city's black community engaged in a brave and unrelenting struggle for equality. Baldwin, an intermittent resident of Savannah throughout his youth, immediately took up the mantle of the movement, his camera acting as a witness to the events unfolding in one of the South's oldest communities. Like photographers across the country, Baldwin was inspired to capture the drama, the violence, and the courage that attended the civil rights movement and led to the passage of the Civil Rights Act of 1964, which outlawed segregation in schools, public places, and the workplace. The photographs Baldwin produced in Savannah document the pivotal events of 1963-64 that culminated in the city's desegregation. His compelling images portray participants in the local movement, both celebrated and nameless; the locations where action occurred, from bars to churches to courthouse; and the events that propelled the movement—protest marches, voter registration drives, and prayer meetings. In addition to their aesthetic value, Baldwin's photos are important historical records that reveal photography's critical role in the documentation of modern life.

Early in its history, the medium of photography was embraced as an agent of democracy and social reform—a tangible means by which the public could gain awareness and understanding. While portraiture constituted the most widespread application of photography during its early history, the use of the camera to document major political events emerged in the mid-nineteenth century. Mathew Brady (1822-96), who described the camera as "the eye of history," captured haunting images of the body-strewn battlefields of the Civil War, one of the first conflicts to be memorialized in photographs. Brady's relentless recording of the unsavory realities of war ultimately led to his financial ruin, but numerous documentary photographers and social reformers would follow him in the quest to record and expose historical events as they unfolded.

Some documentary photographers used their work as a direct means of achieving social reform. Images of immigrants dwelling in overcrowded, dingy tenements in Manhattan, taken by police photographer Jacob Riis (1849-1914) and published in *How the Other Half Lives* (1890), ultimately led to improved housing codes and labor laws. Photographs of child laborers in factories and mills made by Lewis Hine (1874-1940), produced in cooperation with the National Child Labor Committee, revealed the seedy underside of America's rapid industrialization and helped to reform child labor laws. During the Great Depression, the Farm Security Administration charged Walker Evans (1903-75) and Dorothea Lange (1895-1965) with documenting poverty in rural America, resulting in moving images of hardscrabble tenant farm families that helped justify the Roosevelt administration's "New Deal" policy of relief, recovery, and reform.

Photographers began exploring the issue of racial inequality in America decades before the pivotal events of the late 1950s and early 1960s led to the passage of the Civil Rights Act. In 1942, Gordon Parks (1912-2006)—one of the most influential documentary photographers of the twentieth century—shot his famous *American Gothic, Washington, D.C.* (Fig. 1), a portrait of Ella Watson, a custodian in a government building. Parks, a self-taught photographer who grew up poor in a segregated Kansas town, once said, "I chose my camera as a weapon against all the things I dislike about America—poverty, racism and discrimination."[1] The first African American photographer to join the Farm Security Administration (FSA), Parks made his compelling image of Watson following numerous personal encounters with racial discrimination in Washington, D.C. The portrait of the upright yet unassuming figure standing with her mop and broom before a vast American flag has become one of the most profound and enduring visual statements about racial inequality in America.

Memphis-based Ernest Withers (1922-2007), another black photographer closely associated with the civil rights movement, amassed one of the most significant bodies of photographs documenting events in the South. Withers served as an Army photographer during World War II, later joining the Memphis Police Force when it opened its ranks to blacks (who were at that time forbidden to arrest whites). Returning to photography in the early 1950s, Withers worked as a photojournalist for the *Memphis World* and the *Tri-State Defender*. In 1955, he published and distributed a photo pamphlet on the infamous murder trial of Emmett Till, a Chicago boy whose lynching in Mississippi, for the alleged crime of whistling at a white woman, galvanized the civil rights movement. For the next decade, Withers witnessed and recorded pivotal events, including the desegregation of Central High in Little Rock, the funeral of activist Medgar Evers, and the assassination of Martin Luther King Jr. Along the way, he captured less dramatic but equally profound instances of daily resistance, such as William Edwin Jones strolling with his daughter in a protest march in Memphis in 1961 (Fig. 2).

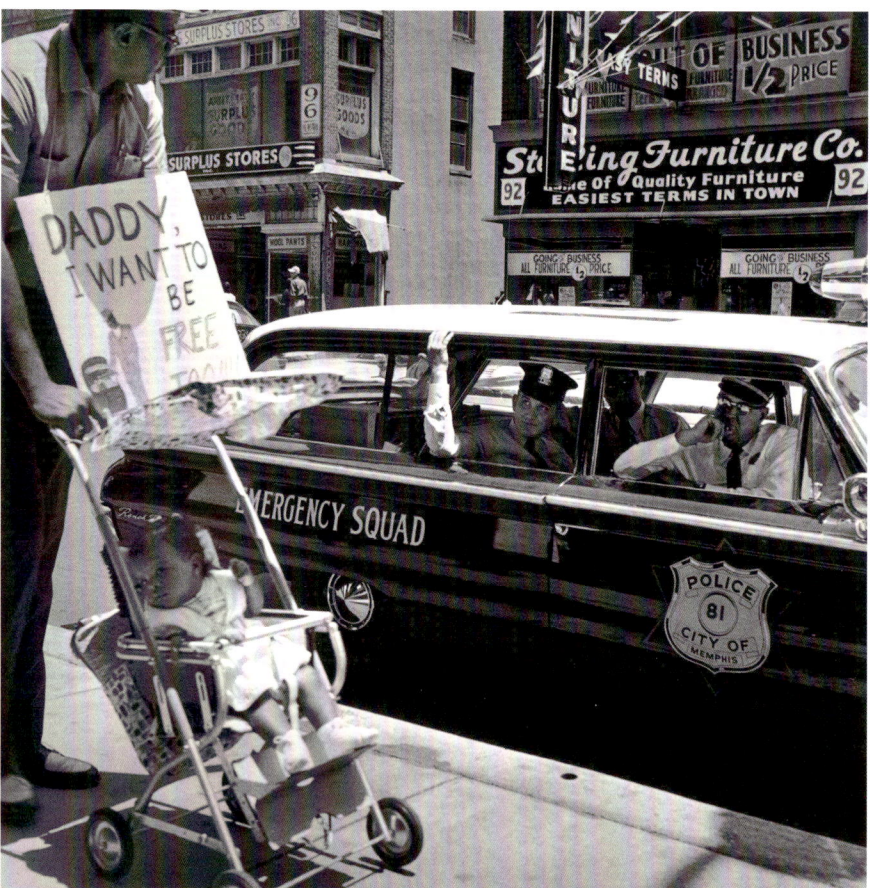

Fig. 2 Ernest C. Withers (American, 1922-2007); *William Edwin Jones pushes daughter Renee Andrewnetta Jones (8 months old) during protest march on Main St., Memphis, TN, August, 1961*, 1961; Gelatin silver print; © Ernest C. Withers, Courtesy Panopticon Gallery, Boston, MA

There were also a number of white photographers who documented the civil rights movement, many of them professional photojournalists. One well-known example is Charles Moore (b. 1931), who, as a 27-year-old photographer with the *Montgomery Advertiser*, was the only photographer on the scene in 1958 when an argument broke out between Martin Luther King Jr. and police officers. His dramatic photographs of King's arrest were distributed by the Associated Press, and one was published in *Life* magazine, where Moore would work as a contract photographer for the next seven years, traveling across the South to reveal the evolving struggle for civil rights. Moore famously captured the brutality on the streets of Birmingham when authorities turned high-powered fire hoses and vicious police dogs on demonstrators (Fig. 3). The widespread dissemination of such images is often credited with turning the tide of public opinion in support of the Civil Rights Act.

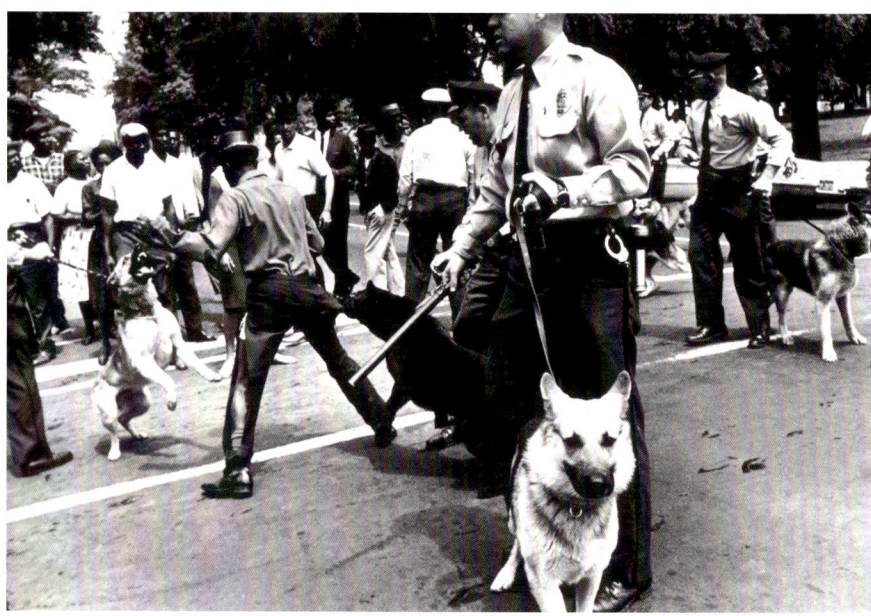

Fig. 3 Charles Moore (American, b. 1931); *A man braces himself as two dogs attack him during racial unrest in Birmingham, Alabama in May, 1963*, 1963; Gelatin silver print; ©1963 Charles Moore-Black Star

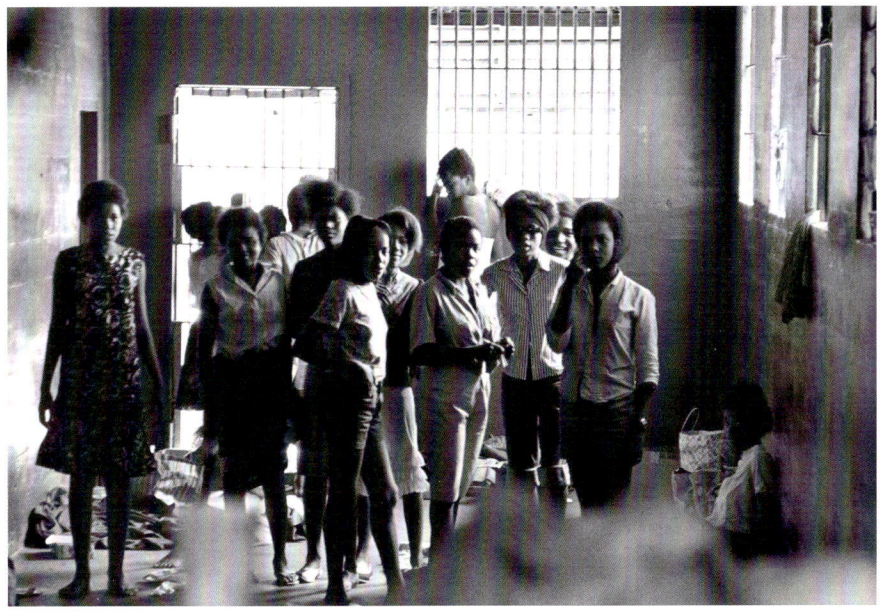

Fig. 4
Danny Lyon (American, b.1942)
Leesburg, Georgia. Arrested for demonstrating in Americus, teenage girls...,No. 10, 1963
Gelatin silver print
©Danny Lyon, Courtesy of Magnum Photos

Danny Lyon (b. 1942), the first staff photographer for the Student Nonviolent Coordinating Committee (SNCC), a national group of college students dedicated to desegregation, traveled the southern and mid-Atlantic states from 1963-64 documenting the civil rights movement. Lyon spent significant time in Georgia, capturing both inanimate manifestations of racism—white versus colored drinking fountains in Albany—as well as mass meetings, sit-ins, and the arrest of protestors in Atlanta. In one instance, Lyon chronicled the plight of over thirty teenage girls apprehended for demonstrating in Americus in 1963 and placed in a stockade near Leesburg, Georgia, without sanitation facilities or beds (Fig. 4). Lyon's photograph is shocking evidence of the inhumane treatment of these young women. Asked in a 1995 interview whether photography really had the power to change things, Lyon replied, "Yeah. I've seen it happen...I took pictures, for instance, of teenage girls in the Leesburg stockade in Georgia. They were virtually starved, held without charges, and I snuck in and took pictures through the bars. The pictures were presented in Congress a week later and the girls were released."²

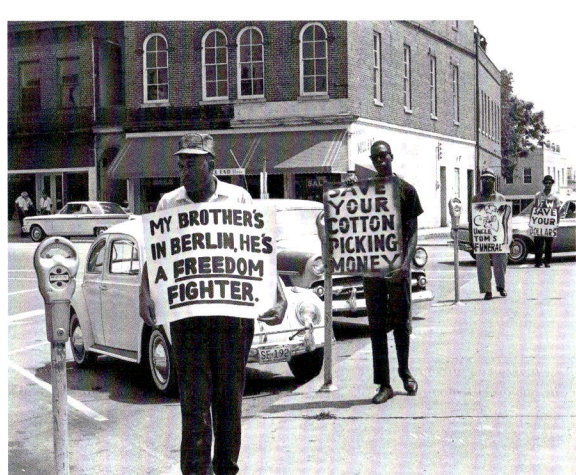

Fig.5
Cecil J. Williams (American, b. 1937)
Picketing in Orangeburg, 1963
Gelatin silver print
©Cecil J. Williams

There were also those photographers in small towns throughout the South who recognized the need to document the struggles occurring in their own backyards. For instance, Cecil J. Williams in Orangeburg, South Carolina, photographed the kinds of events that were happening in towns all over the South: student protest marches, department store boycotts (Fig. 5), sit-ins, and mass meetings. In the case of Orangeburg, Williams also captured a stunning moment of violence in 1960, when police, firemen, and state troopers intercepted marchers and assaulted them with tear gas and fire hoses, afterwards arresting nearly 400 and herding them into a police stockade. Nearly eight years later, the desegregation of Orangeburg had yet to be complete. In what would become known as the Orangeburg Massacre, a civil rights protest staged at a whites-only bowling alley ended in tragedy when police fired into the crowd, killing three and wounding twenty-seven.

Unlike the tragic events in other cities throughout the South, the desegregation of Savannah was largely nonviolent. The process commenced in earnest in 1960, when local students began to stage sit-ins at area lunch counters, and black residents boycotted businesses on Broughton Street that refused to serve or hire them. Photographer Frederick Baldwin began recording local events during the pivotal summer of 1963, when the Chatham County Crusade for Voters, under the leadership of Hosea Williams, began a series of protest marches that were so effective that by the fall of the following year, Savannah was largely integrated. Baldwin's photographs of these events function as a visual summary of the movement in Savannah during the pivotal years of 1963-64.

Frederick Baldwin was born in Lausanne, Switzerland, where his father served as a United States diplomat. He had connections to Savannah through his mother's family, but had lived in the city only intermittently, and never more than two years at a time throughout his youth. After receiving his B.A. from Columbia University in New York, Baldwin returned to Savannah for six months. Although he had no formal training in photography, he was determined to launch a career as a freelance photojournalist. He began, modestly enough, by shooting candid portraits of local children, honing his photography skills while earning enough money to support himself. Baldwin soon moved to Europe in search of more exciting ventures, traveling throughout Sweden, Norway, and France and taking on increasingly significant projects. In 1960, Baldwin led an expedition to the islands of Spitsbergen, located 600 miles from the North Pole, which was sponsored by the New York Zoological Society. There, he took groundbreaking photographs of polar bears underwater that were later published in *Life*. Baldwin returned to Savannah in 1963, after completing his third major Arctic expedition. At the time, he was completely unaware of the burgeoning civil rights movement in the city.

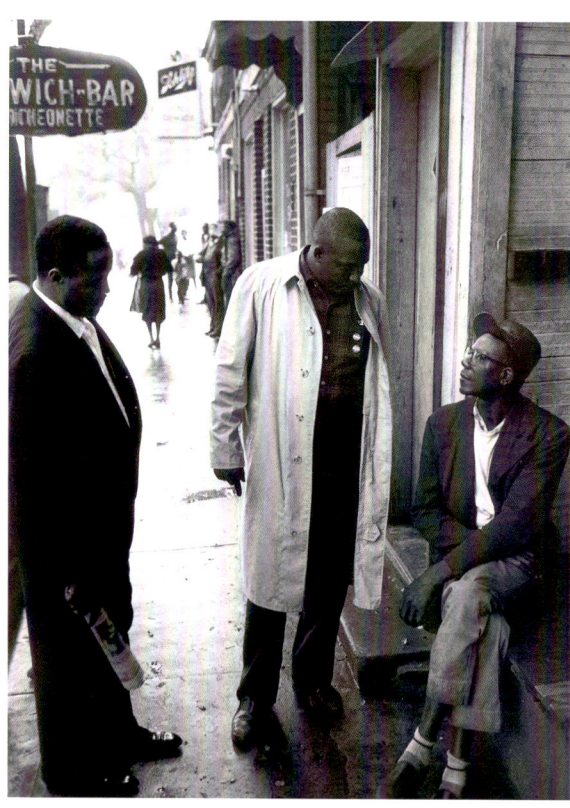

Fig. 6
Frederick C. Baldwin
(American, b. 1929)
"Big Lester" Persuading a Potential Voter, West Broad Street
Gelatin silver print
13 15/16 x 9 1/16 inches
Long-term loan from the artist to the Telfair Museum of Art

Taking stock of the situation, Baldwin soon realized that his family and friends, who were concerned about race relations in the city and eager for a resolution, didn't know much about the organizers on the ground. Baldwin recalls, "I was one of the few white people in Savannah who knew what was going on. I went to meetings, I met Hosea Williams, I was donating my photography to the Southern Christian Leadership Conference. I wasn't significant in the movement—I was useful. They liked me and trusted me—I posed no threat and I provided things they needed."³ When Martin Luther King Jr. came to Savannah in 1964 to speak at the Municipal Auditorium, Baldwin remembers only three white people in the audience including himself and a staff photographer for the local paper. Baldwin's photographs of King addressing the audience represent a high point of the movement in Savannah. Baldwin aptly captures King's calm but determined demeanor and his remarkable skill as an orator, as well as the excitement and anticipation of King's many followers in Savannah.

Baldwin worked with a small, unobtrusive Leica camera that he described as a "passport to take you anywhere." When shooting events on the street, he acted as an inconspicuous observer. In some cases, as when he photographed activist and longshoreman "Big Lester" hauling people out of bars to go register to vote, Baldwin asserts that his presence went essentially unnoticed (Fig. 6). Asked if he considered at the time what significance his photos would have in the future, Baldwin replied, "I just wanted to get it down—I'd deal with it later." For the artist, documenting the civil rights movement was personal—he wanted to record these seminal events in the town to which his family had long been connected. "I knew Savannah. I had worked in a family factory in Savannah with poor whites and poor blacks and saw what was going on in the way my own family exploited their labor—but people were so genuinely kind to me. I never got over that—learning how the other half lives—and the deep sympathy I developed for those workers."

To Baldwin's recollection, there were no other photographers dedicated to documenting the civil rights movement in Savannah. Savannah was not the hotspot. "Unlike other photos of the movement, my work was not showing police dogs or water hoses—it was revealing the interior of what was going on in the civil rights movement. The rest were doing street stuff that would land in major newspapers and magazines." It is precisely this internal aspect of Baldwin's photographs that make them so valuable today; they document the low-key, behind-the-scenes, daily struggle to gain voters, voices, and volunteers. Baldwin depicted the Ballot Bus; the efforts to convince potential voters on the street, in smoky bars, and in Longshoremen's Hall to register; the resulting lines of African Americans registering to vote at the courthouse; protest marches and prayer meetings; and finally, the transcendent moment of Dr. King's visit to Savannah (Fig. 7). Unlike the graphic photos of the violent events in Selma and Birmingham, Baldwin's images reveal the dogged workings of a committed and well-organized group of citizens, fueled by courageous leaders including W.W. Law, Benjamin Van Clark, Andrew Young, and Hosea Williams, and aided by a host of youth willing to sacrifice everything for the cause of freedom.

Despite the lack of overt violence surrounding the civil rights movement in Savannah, moments of tension are revealed in Baldwin's photographs and in the oral histories recorded by community members who personally experienced the city's desegregation. Baldwin captured riot squads equipped with high-powered rifles positioned on the sidelines of a mass meeting; white bystanders with skeptical expressions observing the action; and fearless black marchers holding unequivocal signs with slogans like "Freedom or Death." As Baldwin remembered it, "Savannah was integrated relatively peacefully but for interesting reasons. Savannah considered itself a genteel place—a place where you were kind to the blacks who had brought you up. The elite in Savannah didn't despise the blacks—they despised the Klan, the "white trash"—and they didn't want that kind of déclassé thing going on in Savannah."

Baldwin knew a little about the Klan. Around 1956, when he was supporting himself by shooting portraits of children, he decided to photograph a tobacco auction he had read about in the local paper. On his way to the auction, he drove through Pooler and came across a large gathering of Klan members. He requested permission to photograph them, and spent the remainder of the day shooting their rally on the steps of the courthouse in Reidsville. The incident revealed to Baldwin the depth of the divide between whites and blacks during this period.

Baldwin's experiences photographing the civil rights movement in Savannah profoundly changed his perspective, marking a pivotal point in both his personal and professional development. As he describes it, "I was doing work prior to Savannah that was really ego-driven—exciting, weird underwater pictures that no one had done before—so when I got to Savannah and got involved in the civil rights movement, I got involved with something that was a lot more important than I was. It gradually radicalized me." With this newly acquired sense of purpose, Baldwin left Savannah in 1964 to accept a position with the Peace Corps in Borneo, where he was responsible for supervising 180 volunteers.

Today, Baldwin's photographs serve as potent reminders of the struggle for equality in Savannah, and as evidence of the powerful role of photography in documenting and validating that struggle. As photojournalist Charles Moore pointed out, "Pictures can and do make a difference. Strong images of historical events do have an impact on society. They can help with change."[4] ■

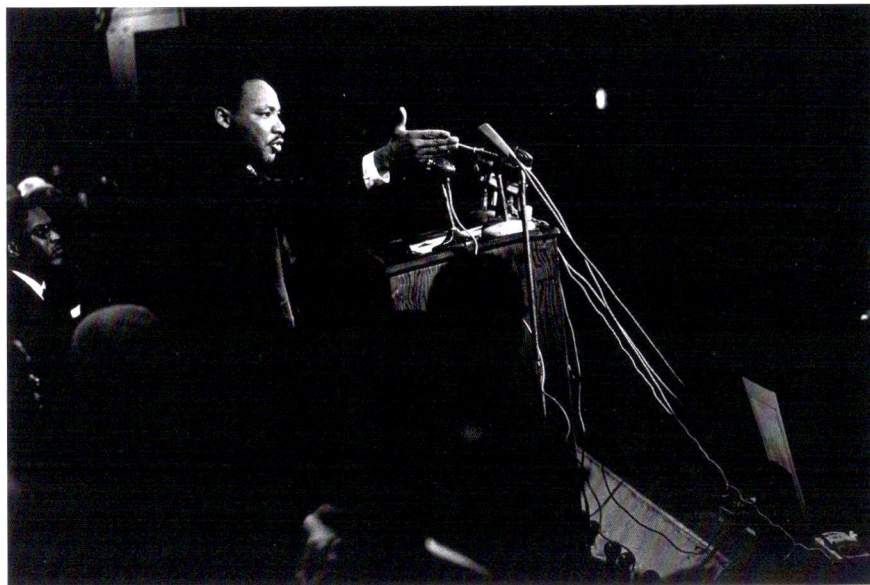

Fig. 7
Reaching Out, Municipal Auditorium, 1964
(See Plate 46)

[1] Gordon Parks, *A Choice of Weapons* (New York: HarperCollins Publishers, 1973).

[2] Nan Goldin, "Doing Life—An Interview with Photographer Danny Lyon," *Artforum* 34 (September 1995): 62-67.

[3] All quotes from Frederick Baldwin were from a phone interview with the artist conducted on June 24, 2008.

[4] Pam Kingsbury, *The Civil Rights Movement from Behind the Lens: An Interview with Charles Moore*, on the Southern Scribe website, www.southernscribe.com/zine/culture/Moore_Charles.htm. June 21, 2008.

Image Plates and Community Recollections

All of the following photographs were taken by Frederick C. Baldwin in Savannah between 1963-64. These works are currently on long-term loan from the artist to the Telfair Museum of Art.

The quotes in this section were excerpted from oral histories provided by community members and individuals active in the local civil rights movement, which were originally recorded in 1983 under the direction of Telfair curator Feay Shellman. The selections that appear here were first published in *"...We ain't what we used to be,"* the catalogue that accompanied the Telfair's 1983 exhibition of Frederick Baldwin's civil rights photographs.

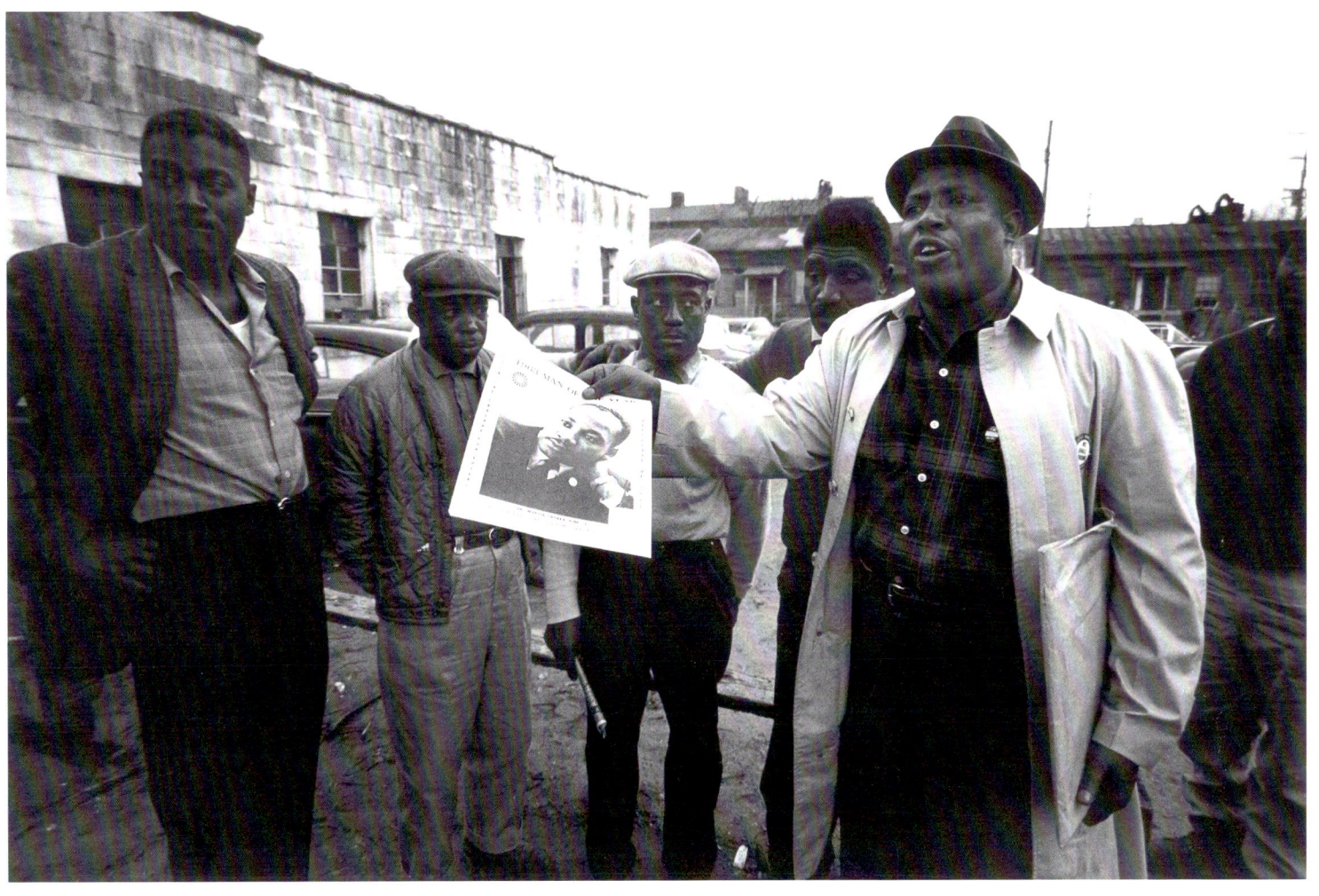

1. **"Big Lester" Among the Longshoremen,** Longshoremen's Hall

Prologue: Racism and Segregation

With such a high density of whites in that area, naturally they had complete control of Daffin Park. Blacks had to either play in the streets or wherever.... They didn't have playground facilities to go to and play and we (blacks) didn't go to Daffin Park to play, but I remember one time—it was my brother and two or three other friends—we were crossing the park, coming from West to East, and these guys (appeared) out of nowhere, it was in the lane, and they jumped out of the trees around us. And they outnumbered us greatly. And they were larger than us, but, there were two larger white guys in Daffin Park playing golf, hitting golf balls, and they saw what was happening and they ran the guys off. (We) were just kids and (they) were much larger teenagers.

—Henry Dingle

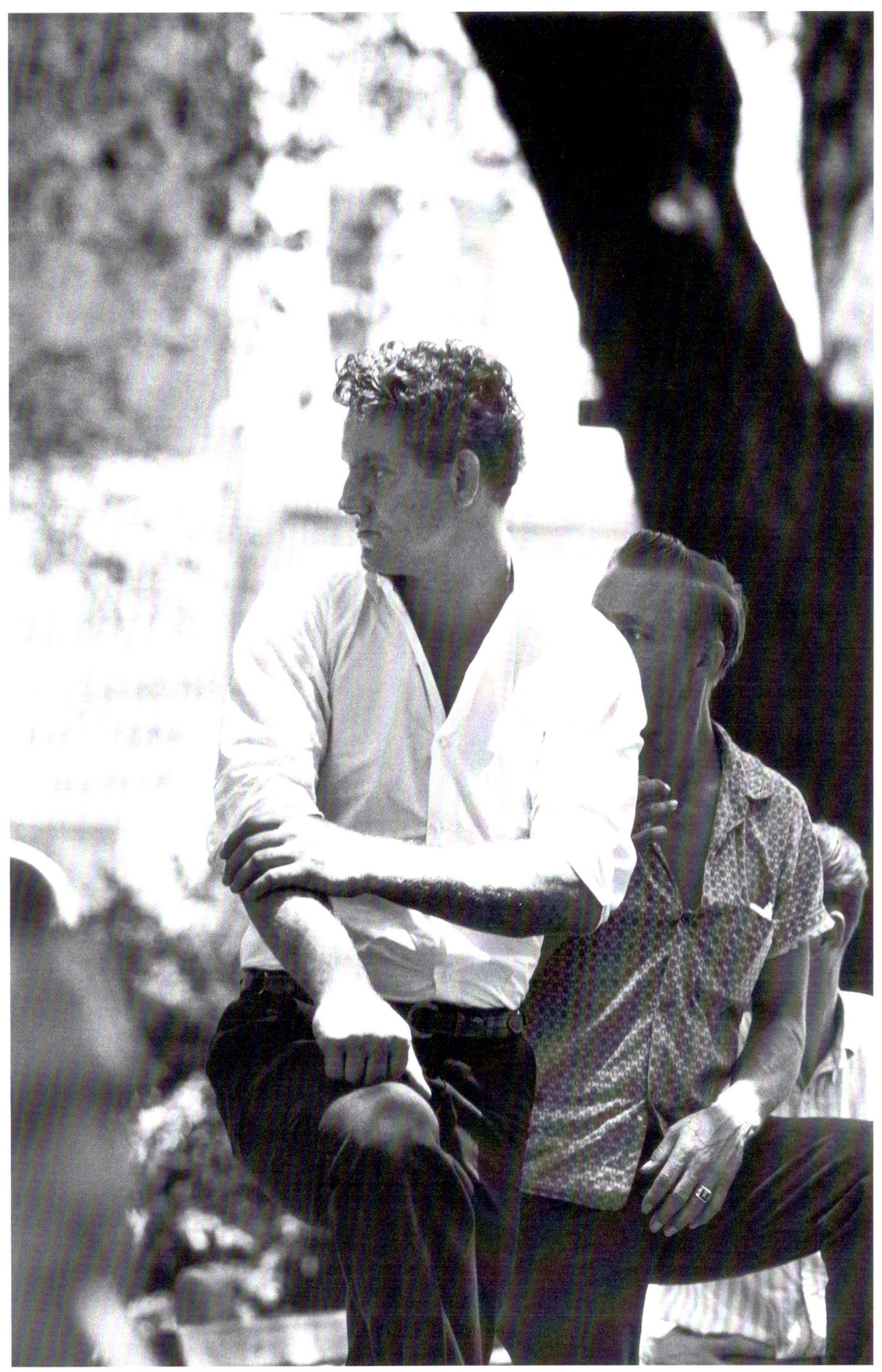

2. Bystanders, Wright Square

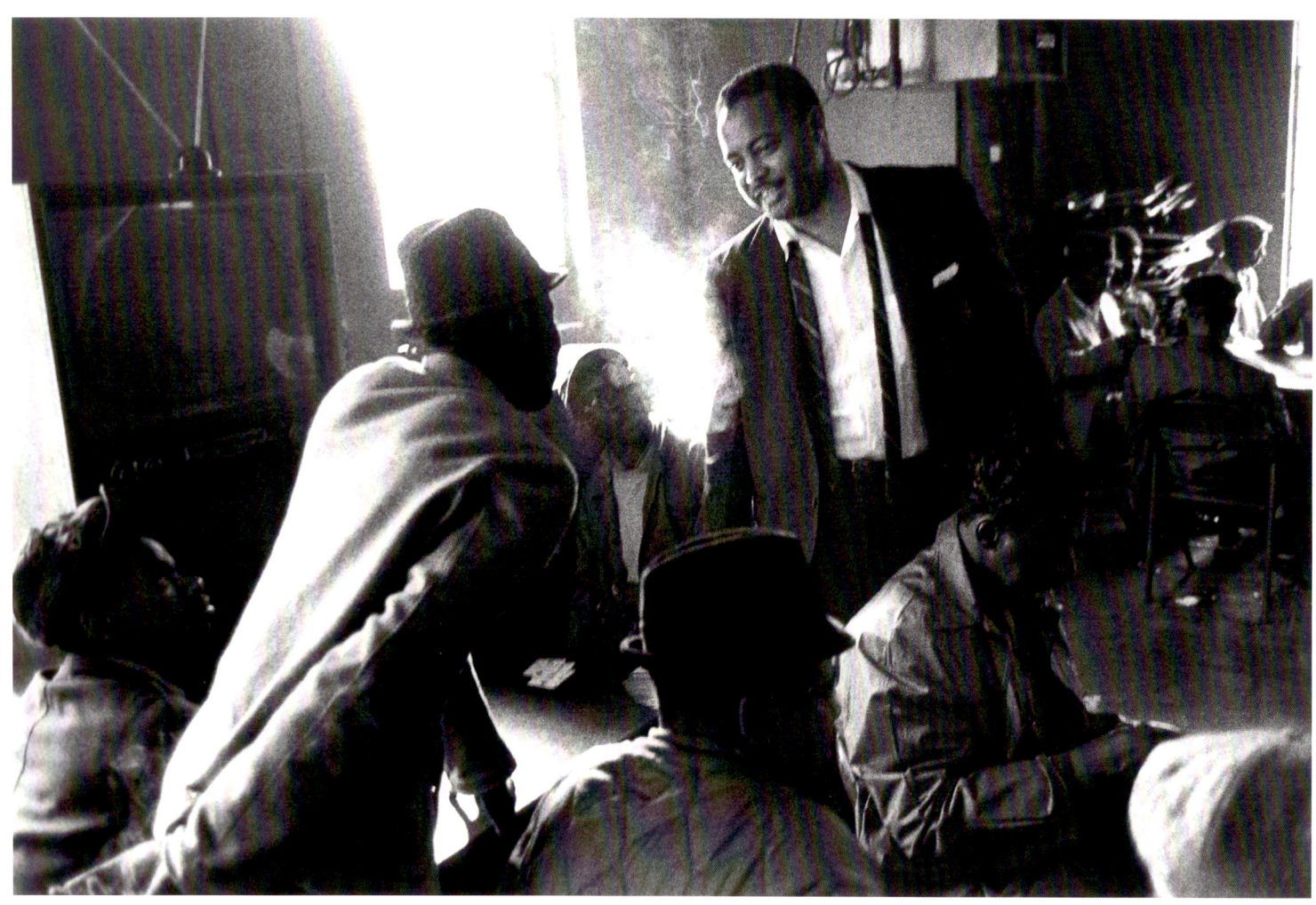

3. Hosea Williams, Longshoremen's Hall

He (Hosea Williams) was in a foxhole with a direct hit and everybody else in the foxhole was killed in Germany. He was in the hospital…thirteen months or so, comes back a World War II veteran on crutches, and drinks from a water fountain—the only water fountain in the bus station where it had a white sign over it—and he got roughed up. And he decided the he wasn't going to fight for democracy in Germany and almost die and then come back to Georgia and not be able to get a drink of water because he was black. Now, that kind of, that was a new phenomena that NAACP had not yet incorporated. This emerging new class of veterans.

—Andrew Young

I was born and I grew up on a farm outside of Minneapolis. It was quite a move for me because I had never been away from home before I came here. I was twenty and it was perhaps one of the greatest transitions I guess that one could have made because I really didn't know that there were places like Savannah, and I'll admit that I thought maybe I wouldn't stay when I first got here. But the people were so friendly and then, my father had cautioned me about leaving a job too soon….I guess that's why I stayed the first year and then after I'd been here for a year and I became fond of the people, you know, and I liked my work and all and I stayed. And then, the third year I was here I got married and that sort of (sealed it). Almost, until my daughter was born, and then I wanted to leave, sure enough. I just couldn't see her growing up in that atmosphere. I just couldn't. Even as she grew, it was so painful.

We'd go downtown and she'd want to get a drink of water, you know, and I'd have to tell her no, she couldn't. She'd see the other children drinking water and I couldn't explain to her why she couldn't drink water too. You couldn't go to the bathroom, you couldn't, oh it was just, it was really horrible. It was really horrible.

—Martha W. Wilson

Voter Registration

All I wanted to do was get people registered. 'Cause I knowed if we could get enough people to vote, we could change things. That's what it was going to take to change. We didn't want to fight nobody. We wanted things changed. We wanted to change it right. We weren't up to no trouble…What we did, we walked from door to door. That's the way you have to do it. Me and my wife and several more other people, we walked from door to door asking people to vote, go down and register. I took my car. I bet you I must have hauled more than 500 to the poll myself.

—James C. Middleton Sr.

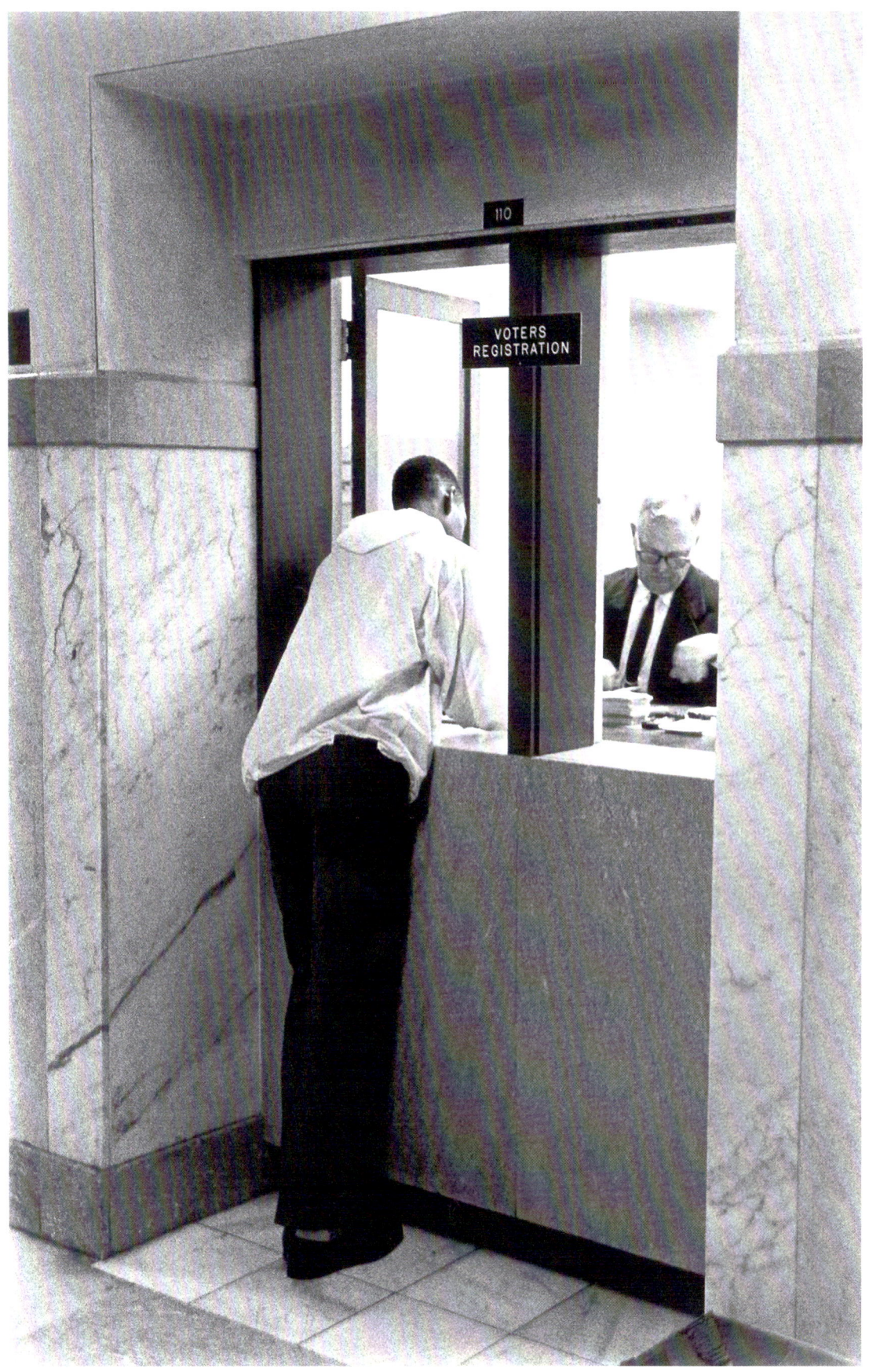

4. The Registrar, Chatham County Courthouse

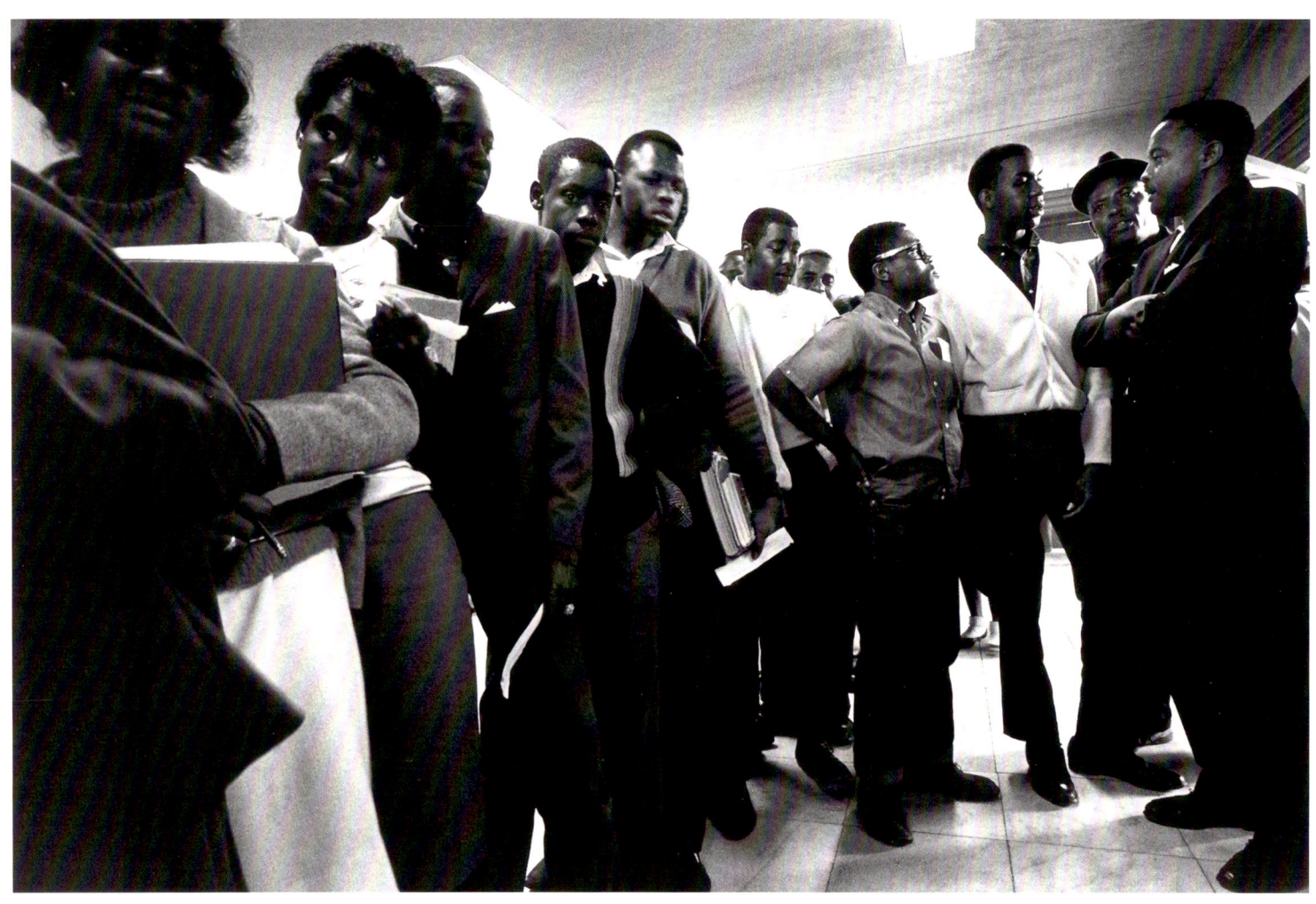

5. High School Students Waiting to Register, Chatham County Courthouse

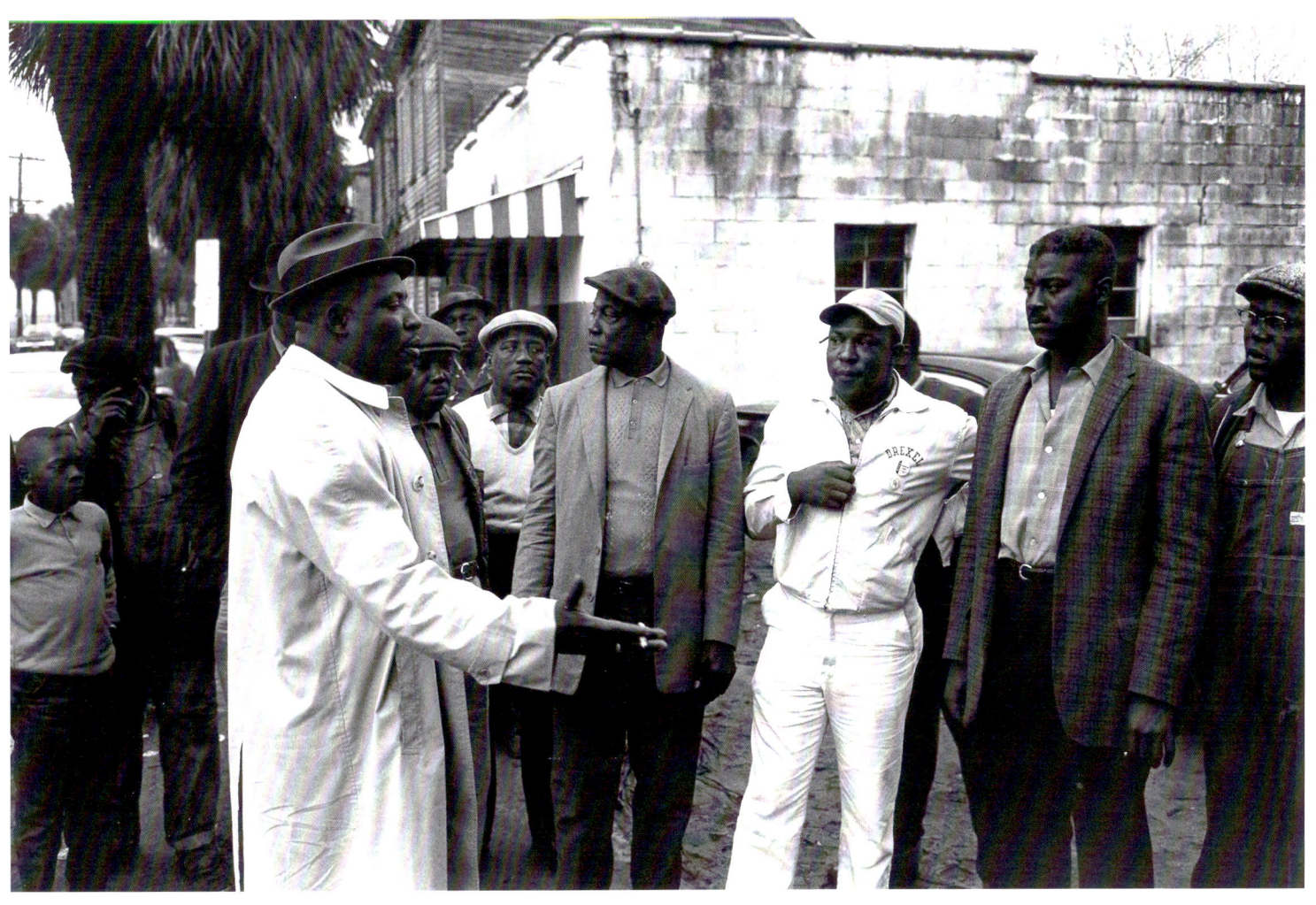

6. "Big Lester" and "Trash" Recruiting Longshoremen, Longshoremen's Hall

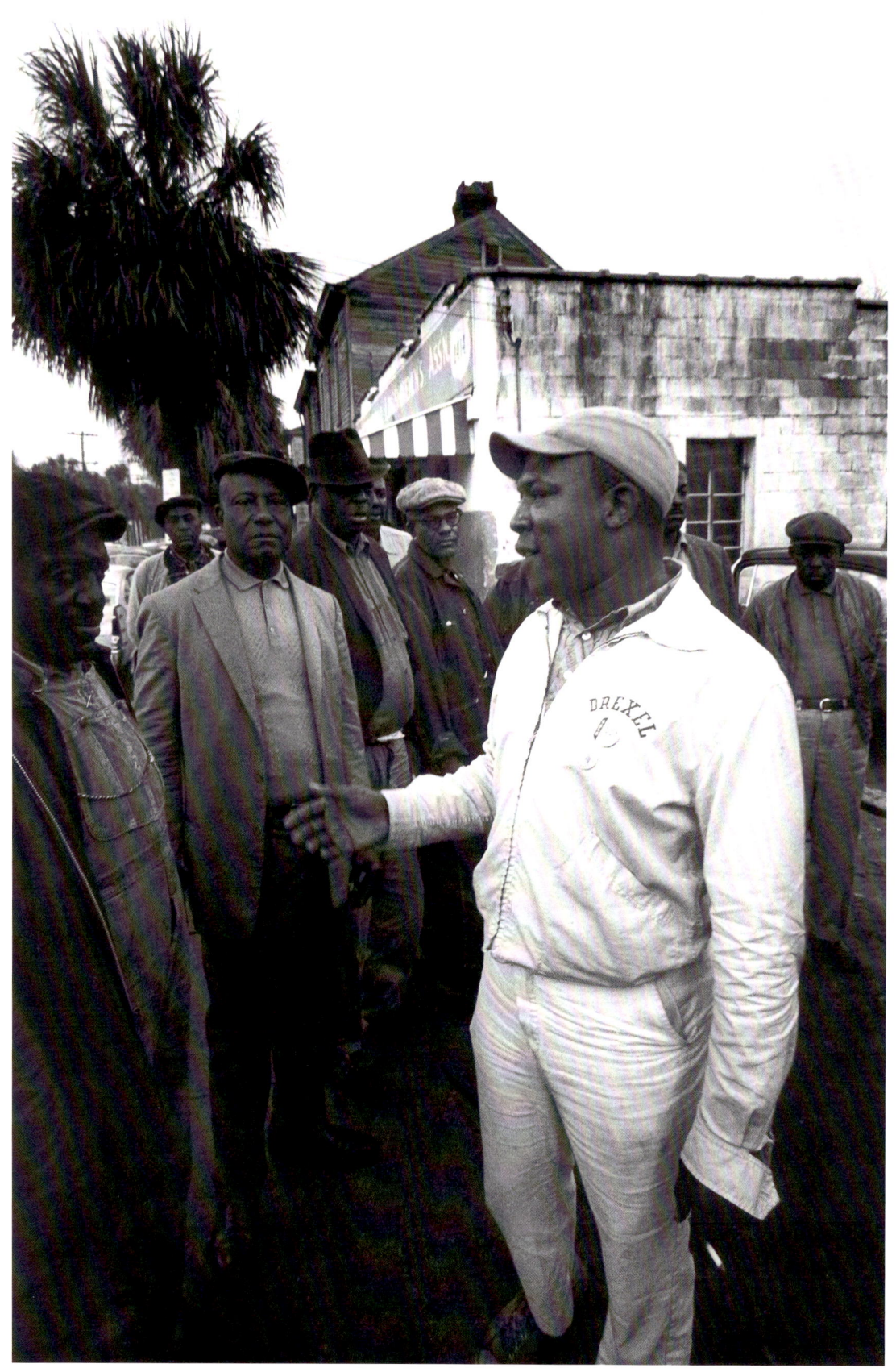

7. "Trash" with Longshoremen, Longshoremen's Hall

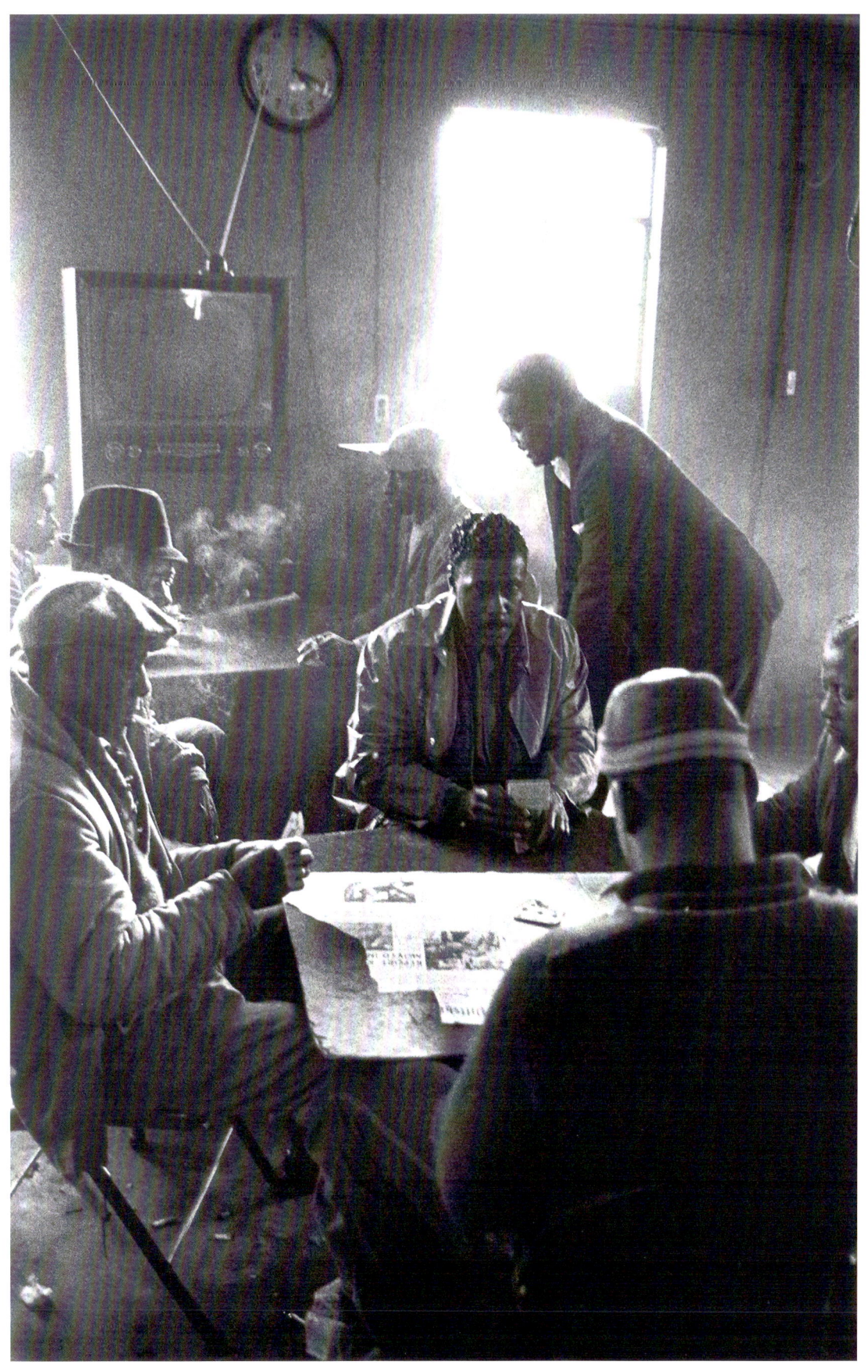

8. Hosea Williams Preaching Voter Registration, Longshoremen's Hall

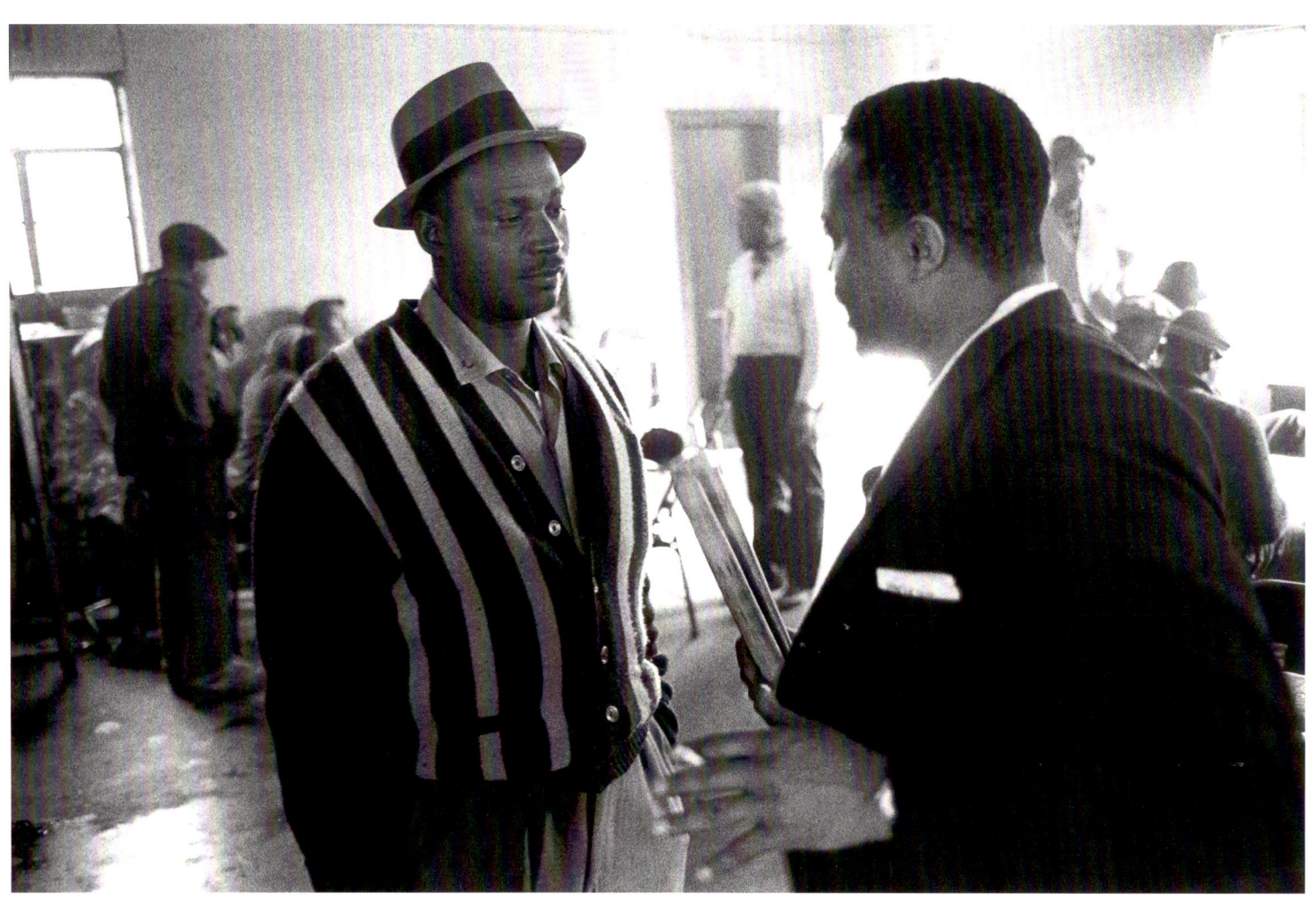

9. **Hosea Williams Discusses Voter Registration,** Longshoremen's Hall

The Registrar got me interested, really interested. You know, they told me, they came by the house, came knocking on the door (and) say, "How about going to get registered?" To me, it was just something to do, that first thing. But after she (the Registrar) start treating me like I wasn't nobody, then I was determined to become a registered (voter). Then I start looking up on it and finding out that I wasn't even a citizen, not being registered.

So then, from her turning me back, it really made my ego go higher. Because, then I got interested, and after the fourth time I went and checked it out and (they) said if you not a registered voter, you're not a citizen, so I said, 'Hey, this is my native home. I'm not even a citizen in my home." So then, you know, from her making me go back, and talking to Mr. Law and Mr. Hosea Williams, and, you know, finding out I was not really a citizen unless I become a registered voter…these are the things that prompt me to continue fighting. But first thing when I went down to sign, it was just because a group came to my house and knocked on the door and say get registered…Now, her (the Registrar) saying that you not qualified to register or you didn't read like I want you to read, it got me to the point that I want to push more. So then I got involved in a lot of more things that I wouldn't have gotten involved in.

It changed my whole outlook in life. My whole life. My whole life was a turning point from that day when I had to fight seven times to get registered.

—Frances Bright Sanders

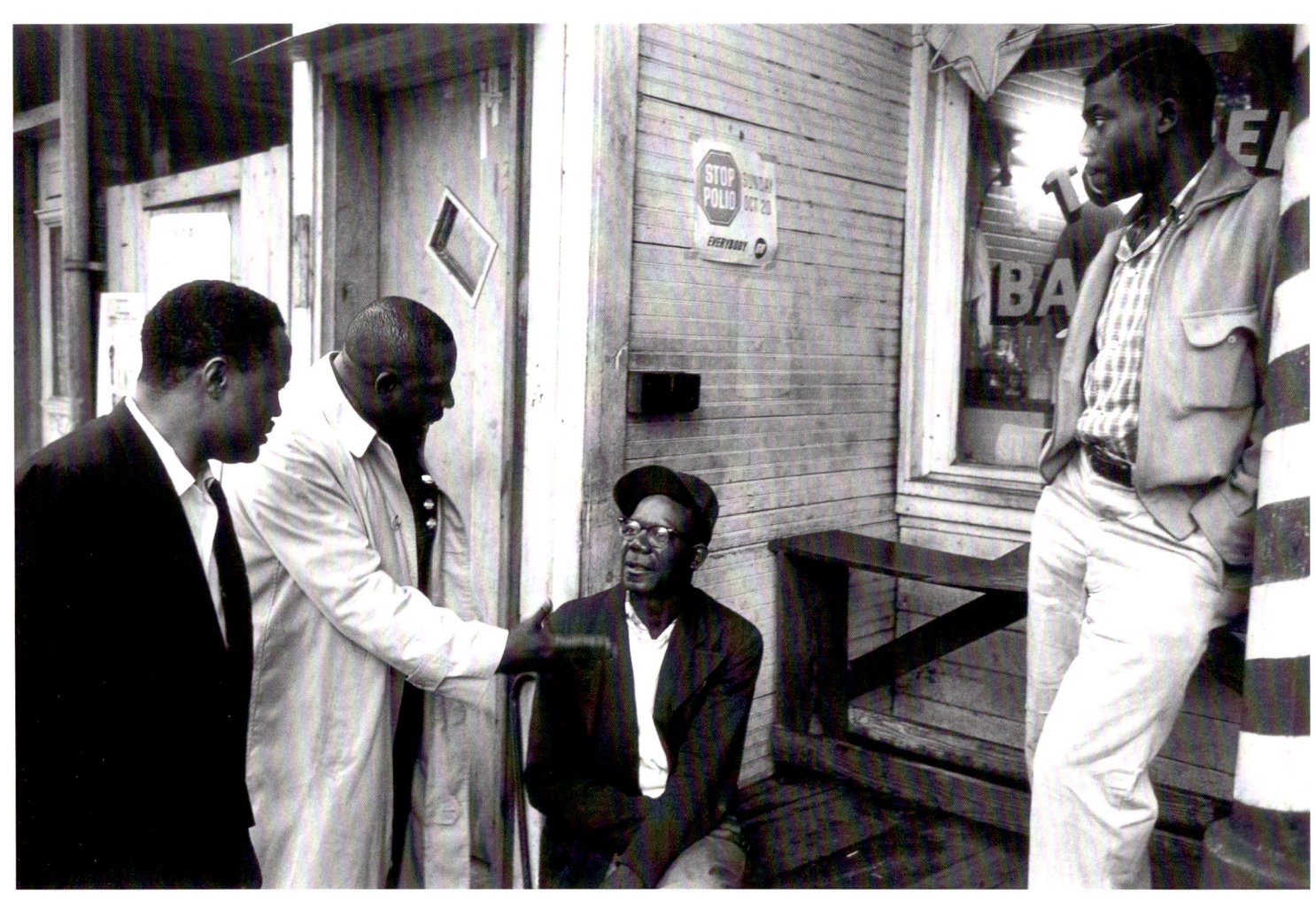

10. Skepticism, West Broad Street

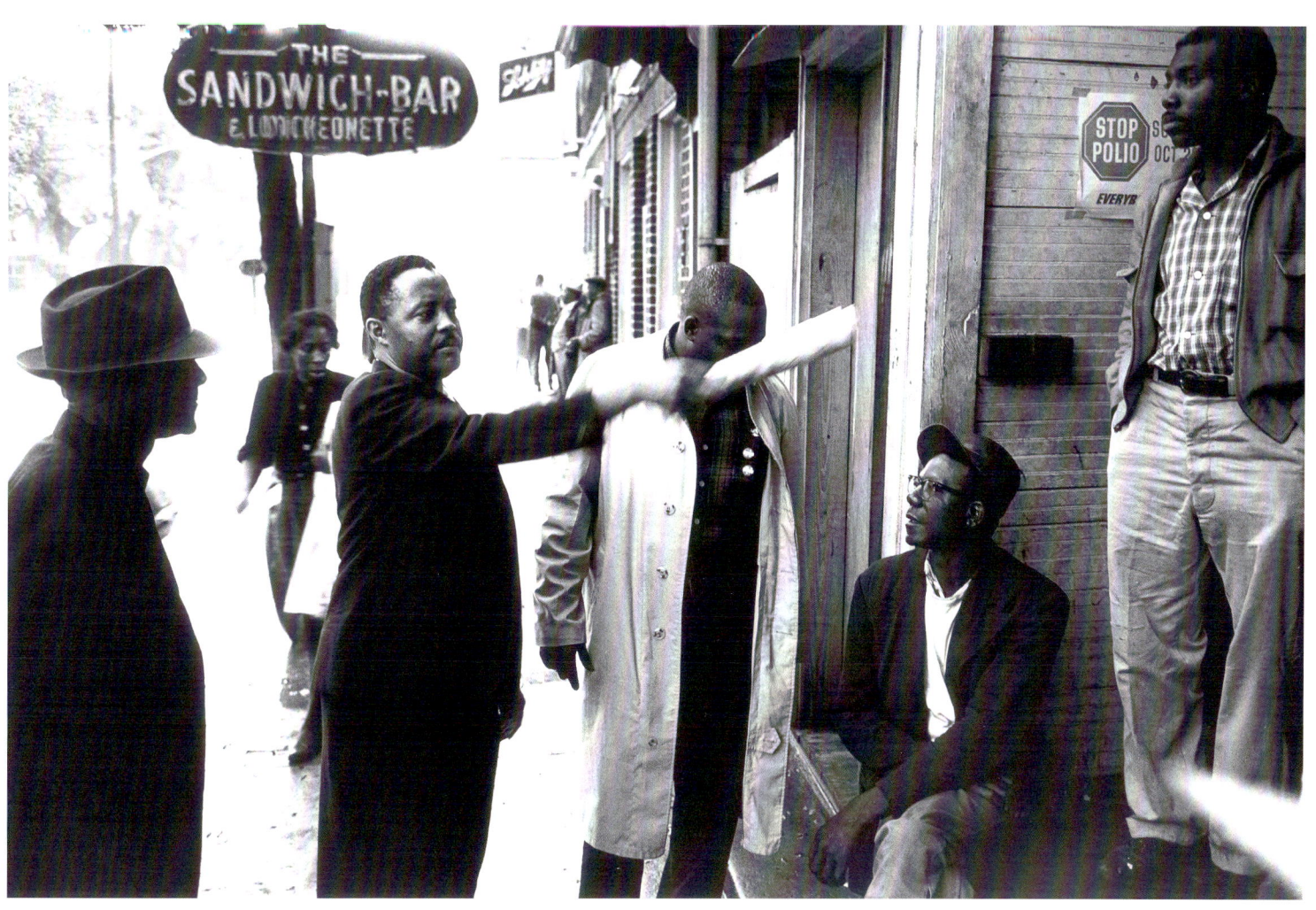

11. Persistence, West Broad Street

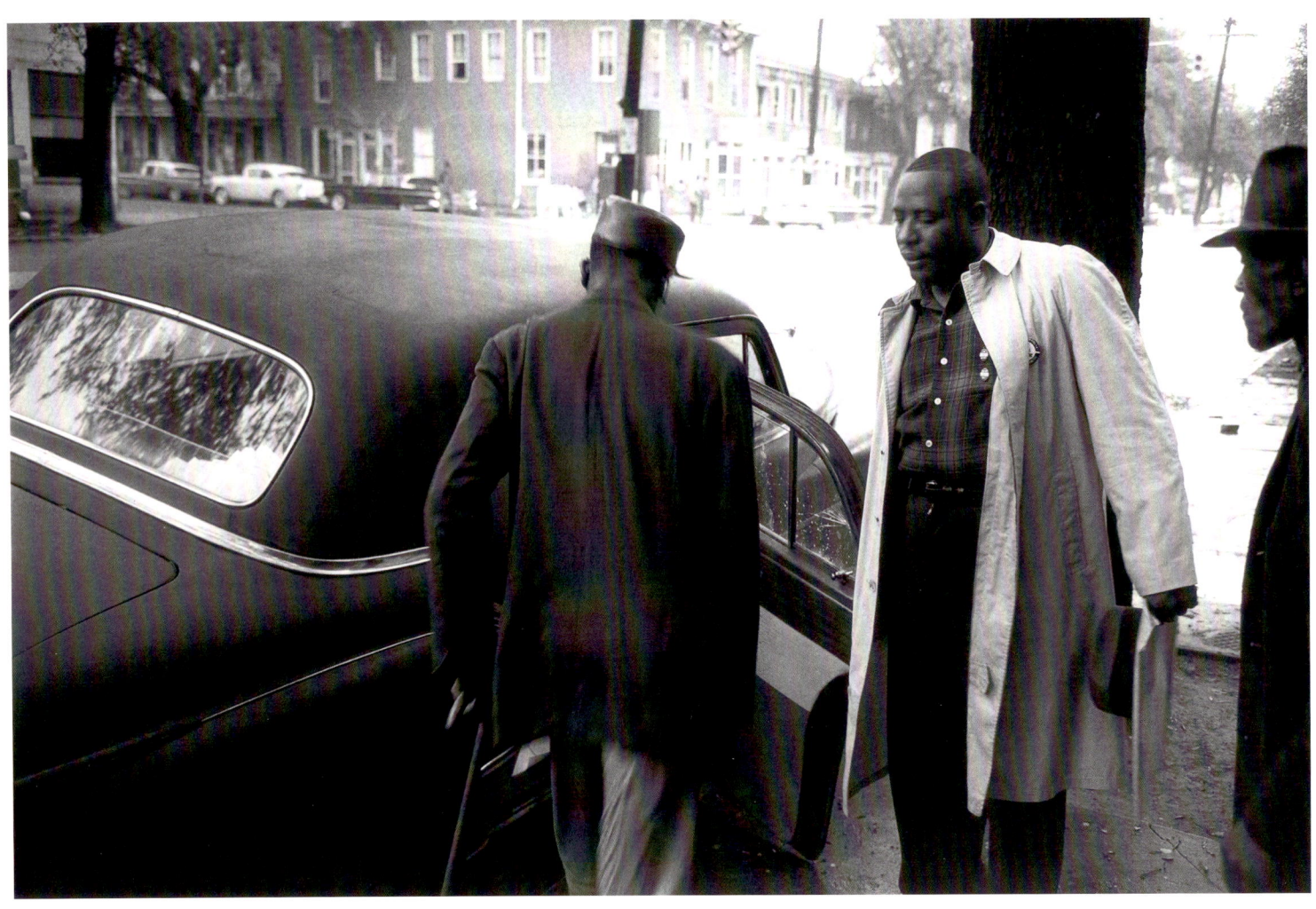

12. Success, West Broad Street

Lester was pretty good at that. Lester would dress you, Lester would dress you. "Come on old man, come on, come on, where did you say your pants at? In here? All right, come on,…very good, okay, you don't need a hat on, everything good." I remember this instance. We went to this house and it was an old couple and they wanted to go, but then for fear that their life would have been in jeopardy. Well, the old lady, she had a job, but she was working for some whites. She said, "Well, if she find out that I go (register to vote), she might fire me." Lester said, "Don't you worry, I got a job for you." She said, "What kind of job?" He said, "I'm going to let you drive the bus (the Ballot Bus)."

—Nathaniel N. Boles

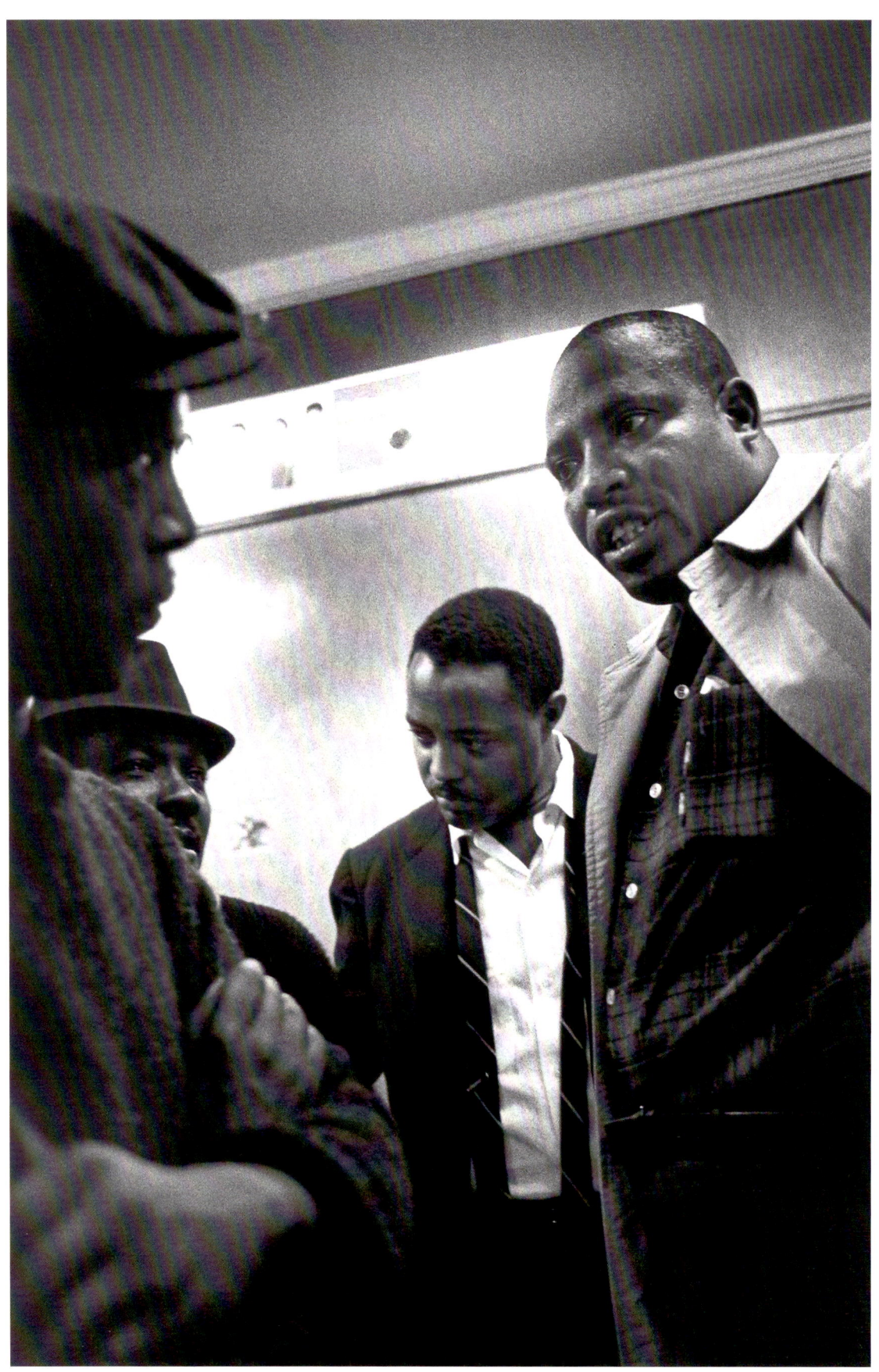

13. "Big Lester" Makes a Point

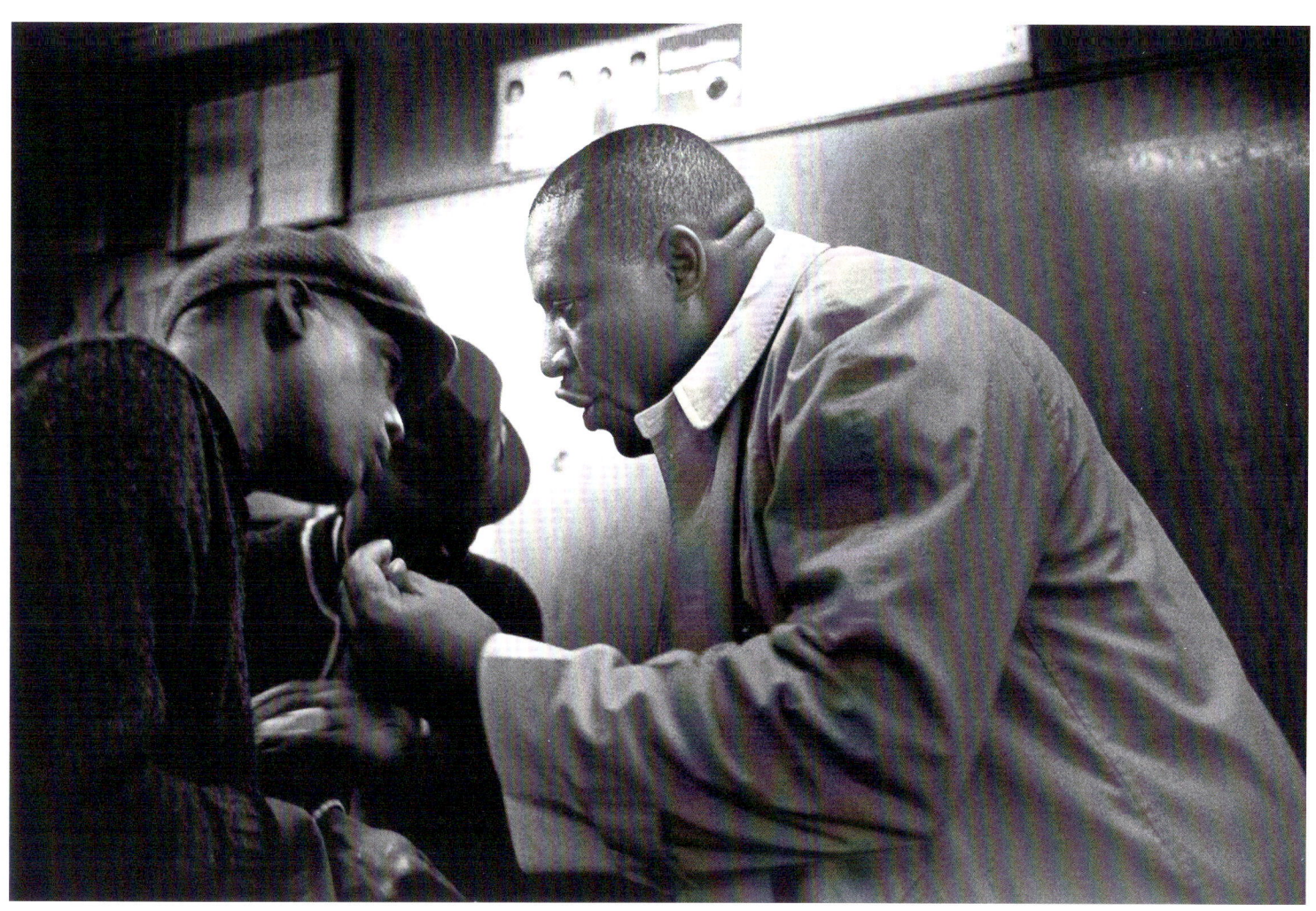

14. "Big Lester" Captivates

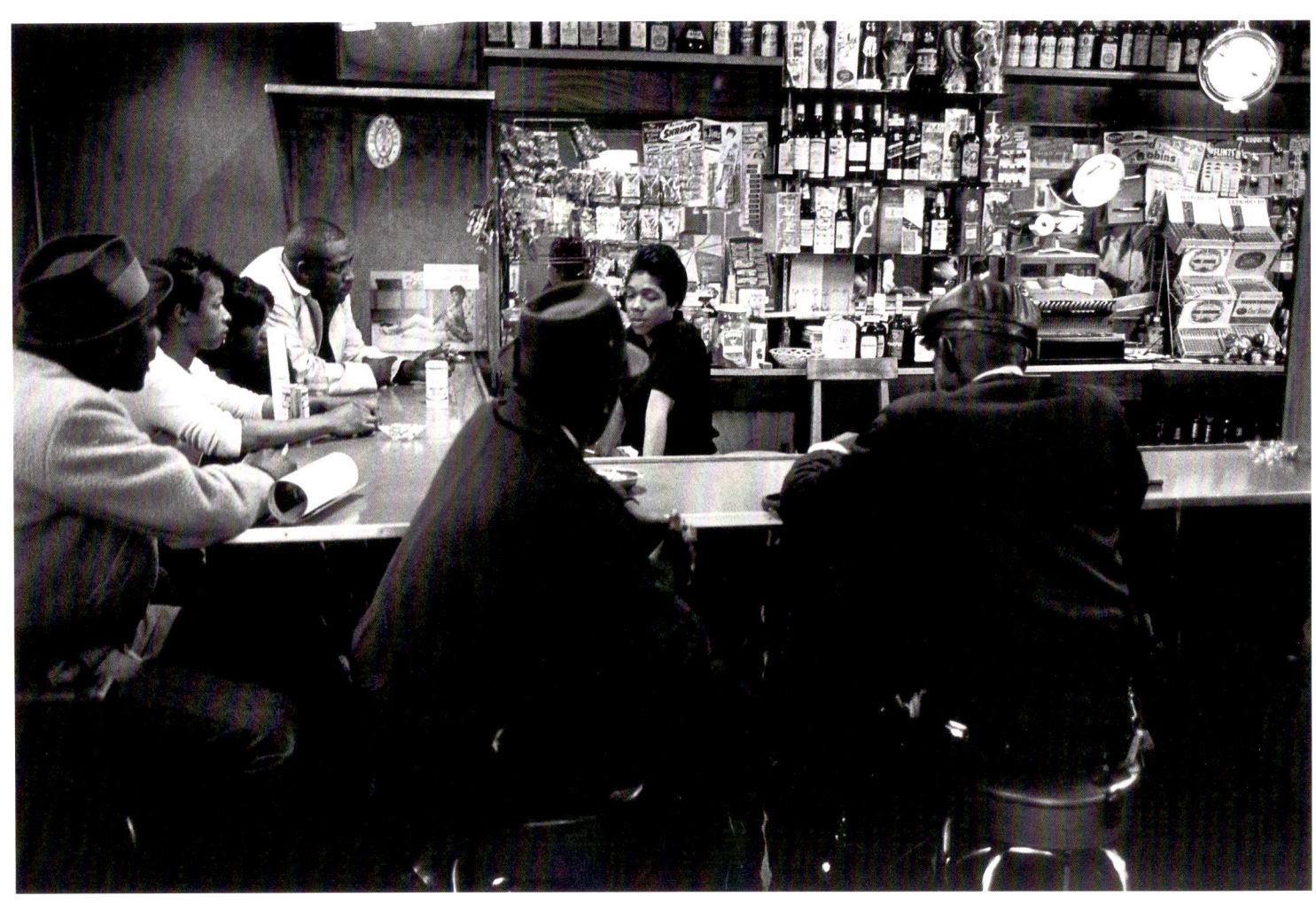

15. "Big Lester" Persuades the Patrons, West Broad Street

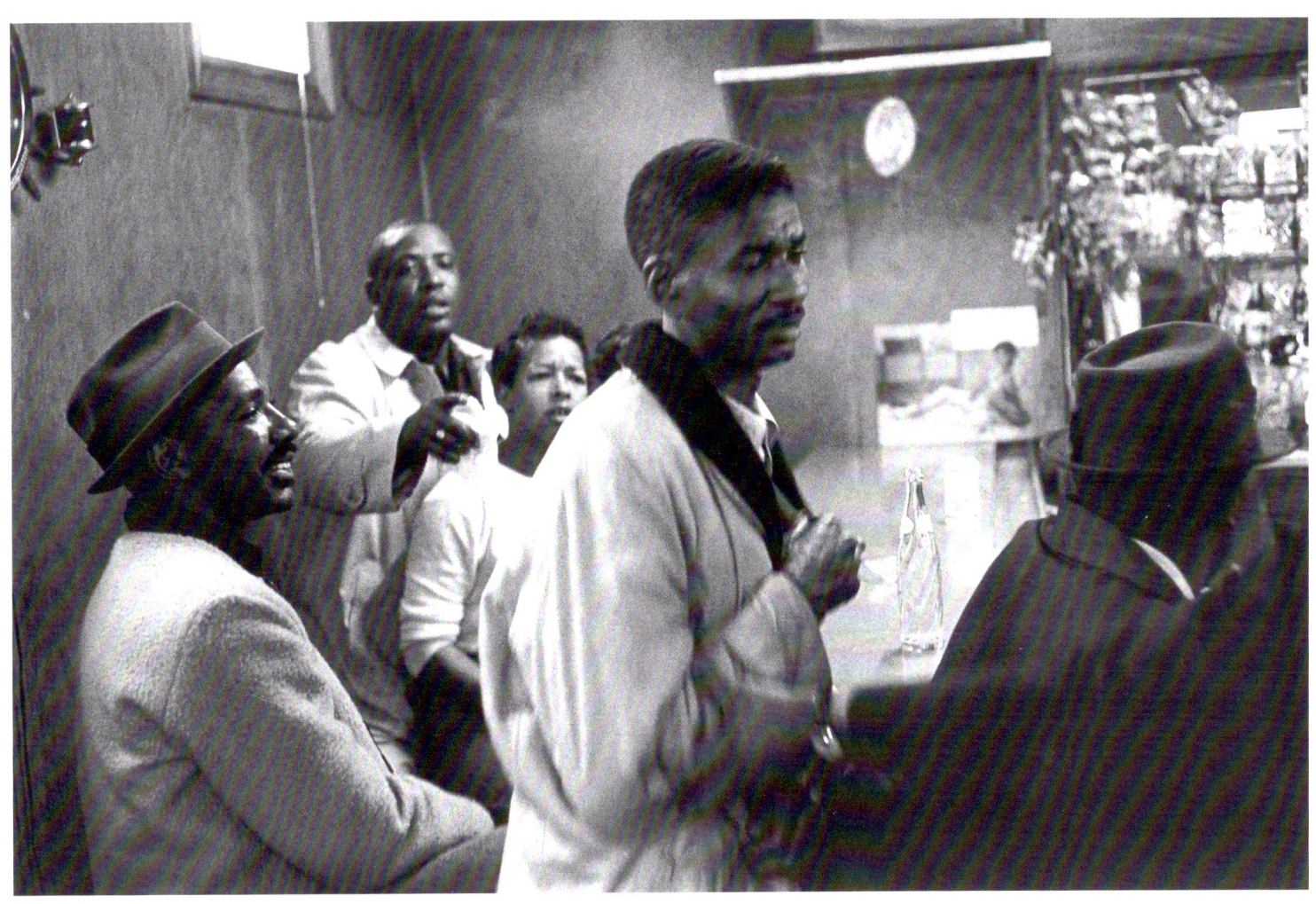

16. **No One Escapes Lester,** West Broad Street

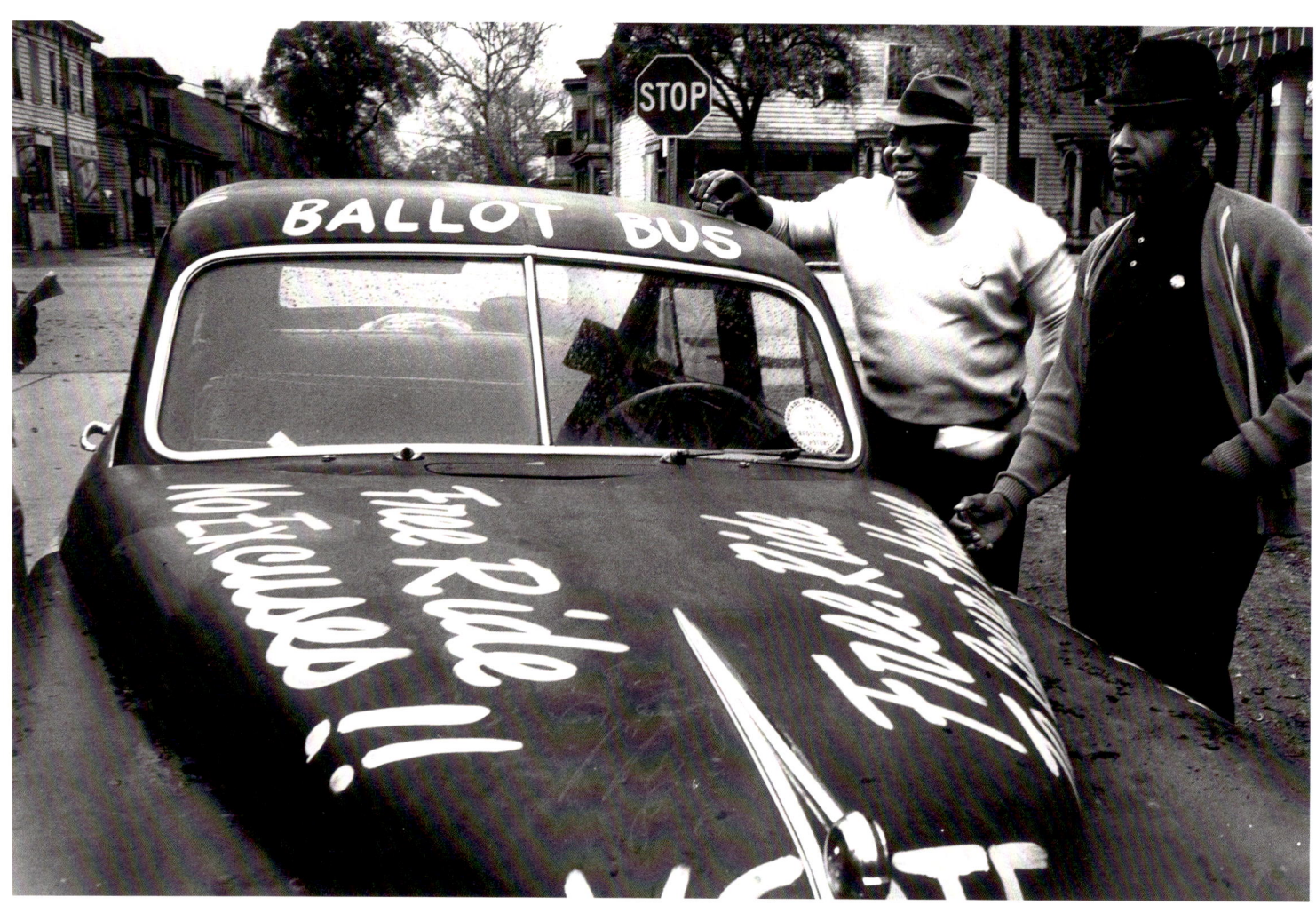

17. The Ballot Bus

The Chatham County Crusade for Voters: Leadership, Organization, Strategy

Oh gosh, what didn't we do? We had to keep up with all the members who belonged to the Crusade for Voters, all the participants in the movement to a degree. We had to make sure on many occasions that they were fed when they were hungry…We started a little newspaper and, of course, that had to be laid out. All the typing that had to be done, we'd do. We would go out and solicit funds as a means of survival.* These contributions were tax-deductible, from community businessmen. And that was my job.… I had to go out and do that. Well, my job was more than just being the secretary. We all did everything in order for the civil rights movement to work in Savannah. And I mean something as simple as somebody needing a ride, or if they needed money to catch a cab.* I mean all the little things we had to do in order to keep the whole thing together, because it might have been a small part but it was an important part. All of the small bits made up the whole. So in my opinion, no one in the movement was unimportant. Everybody was important and we tried to make them feel that way, which they were and they still are, because if they were not there, a piece of the puzzle would have been missing.

—Carolyn Roberts Barlow

*Where * appears interviewees elected to edit their own quotes.

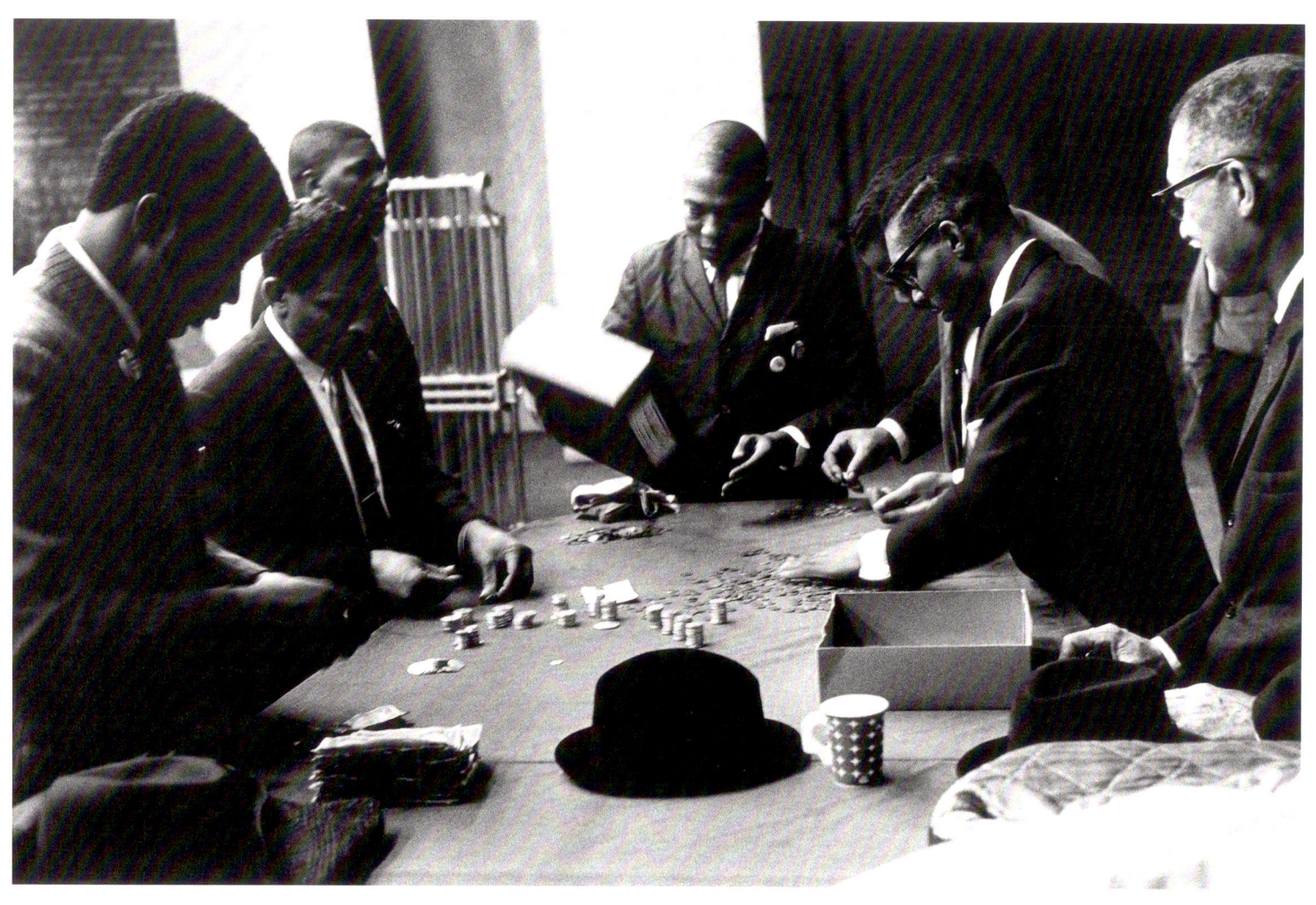

18. Counting Contributions

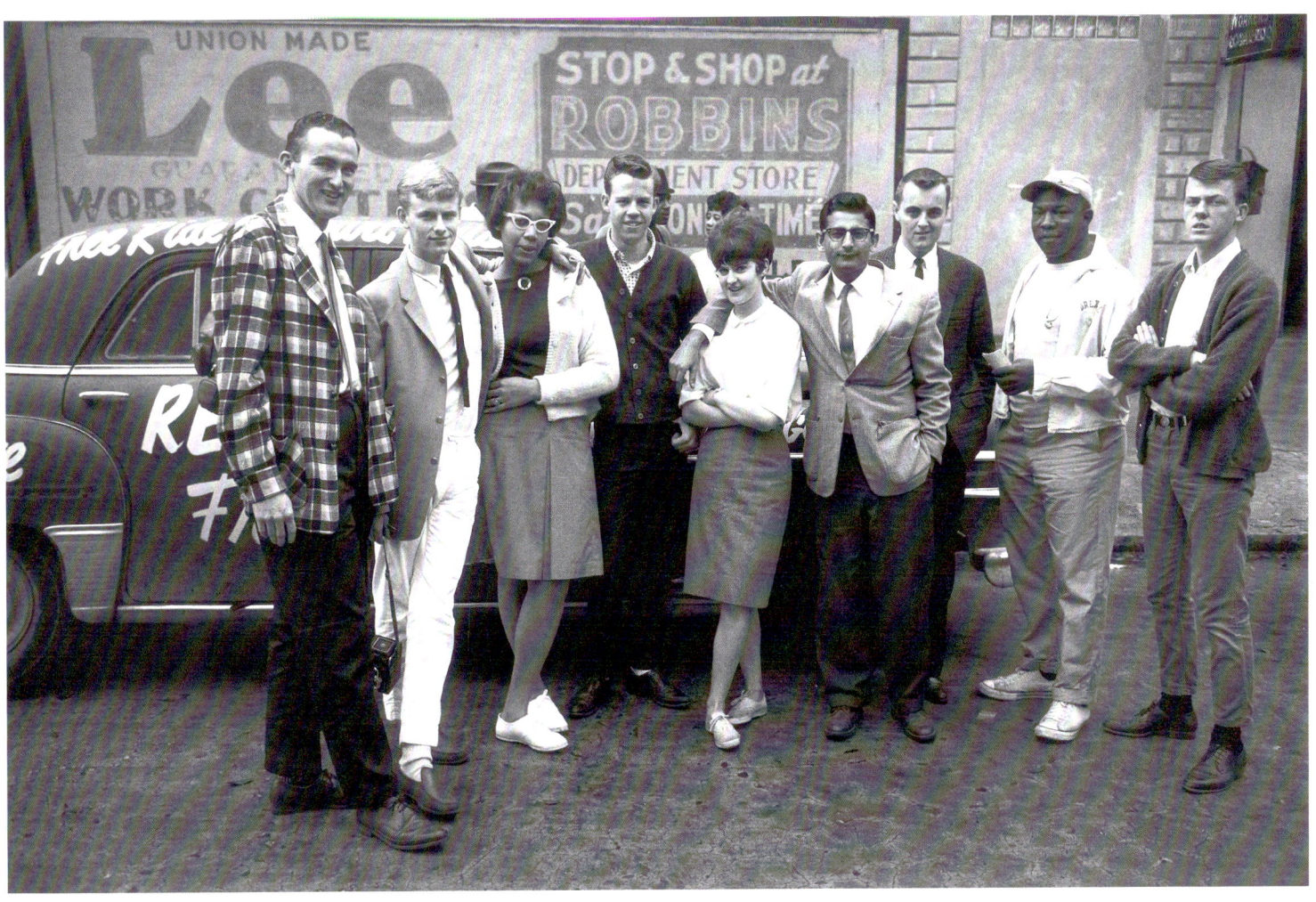
19. Civil Rights Workers Posing with Ballot Bus

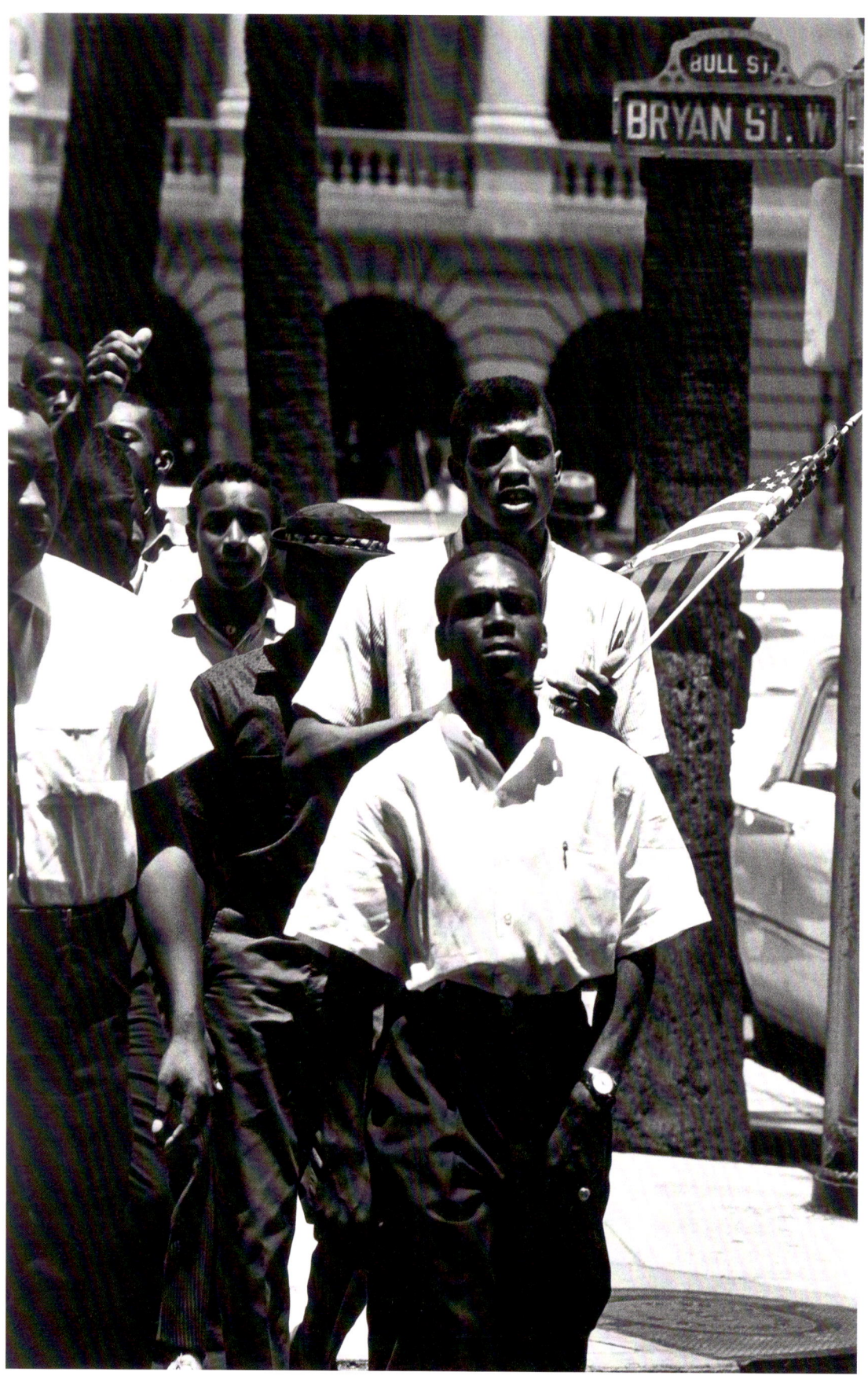

20. Benjamin Van Clark Leading a March, Bull Street

Basically, what we would do before any meeting or any march, we would sit down with what we called our leadership, you know. We might get the captain of the baseball team, the captain of the football team, or something—people who knew how to work with people. And we would preach nonviolence into them so much until when they get on the street, all they knew was nonviolence. 'Cause we talked to them about this and that, we teach them (the) route, and when we get downtown, if you (are) the head of the line and somebody (is) at the back of the line, they know what the head of the line is doing, 'cause we teach in the beginning. We just never go out and say, "Come on and lets go and we going to do this and we going to do that."

—Benjamin Van Clark

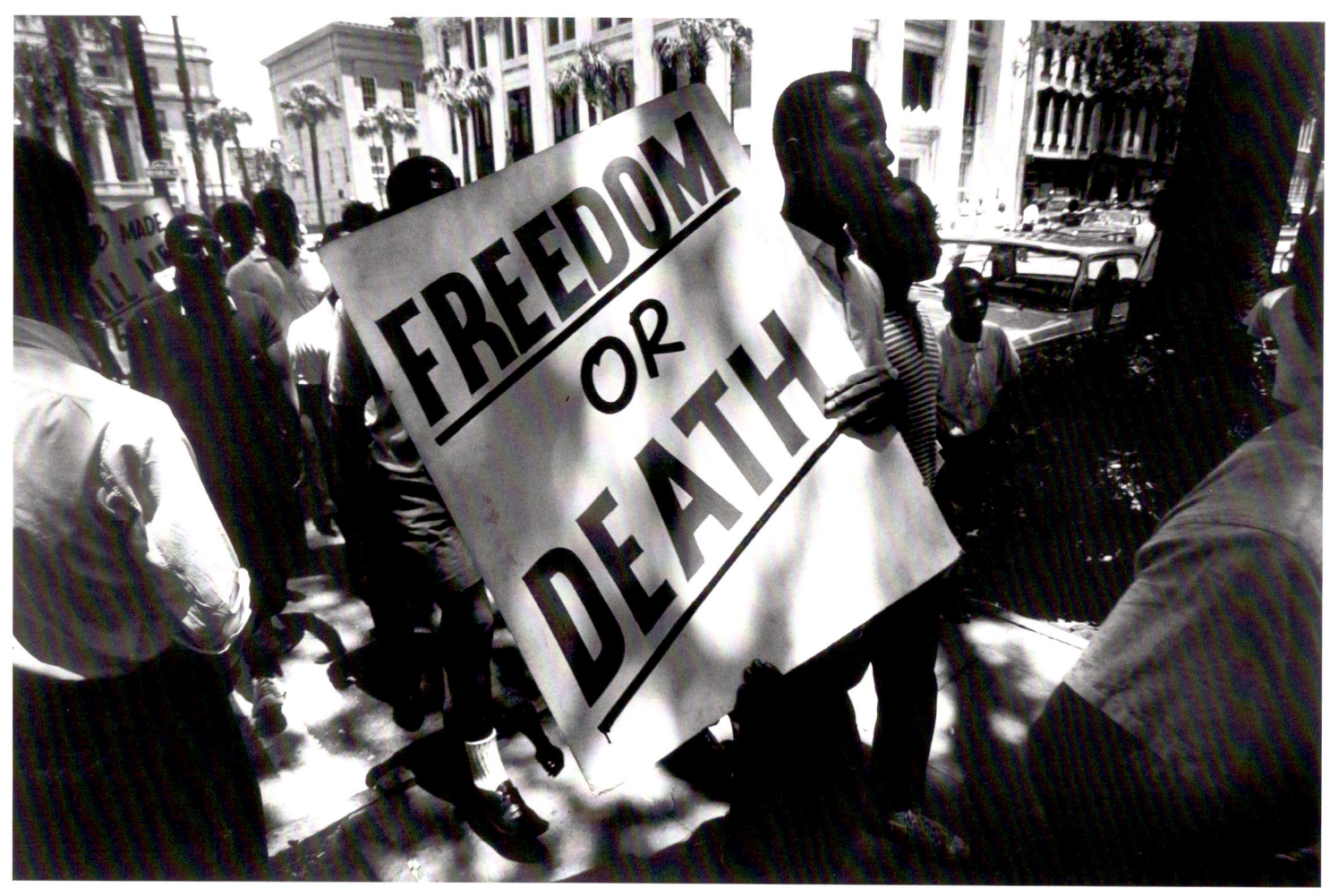

21. Freedom or Death

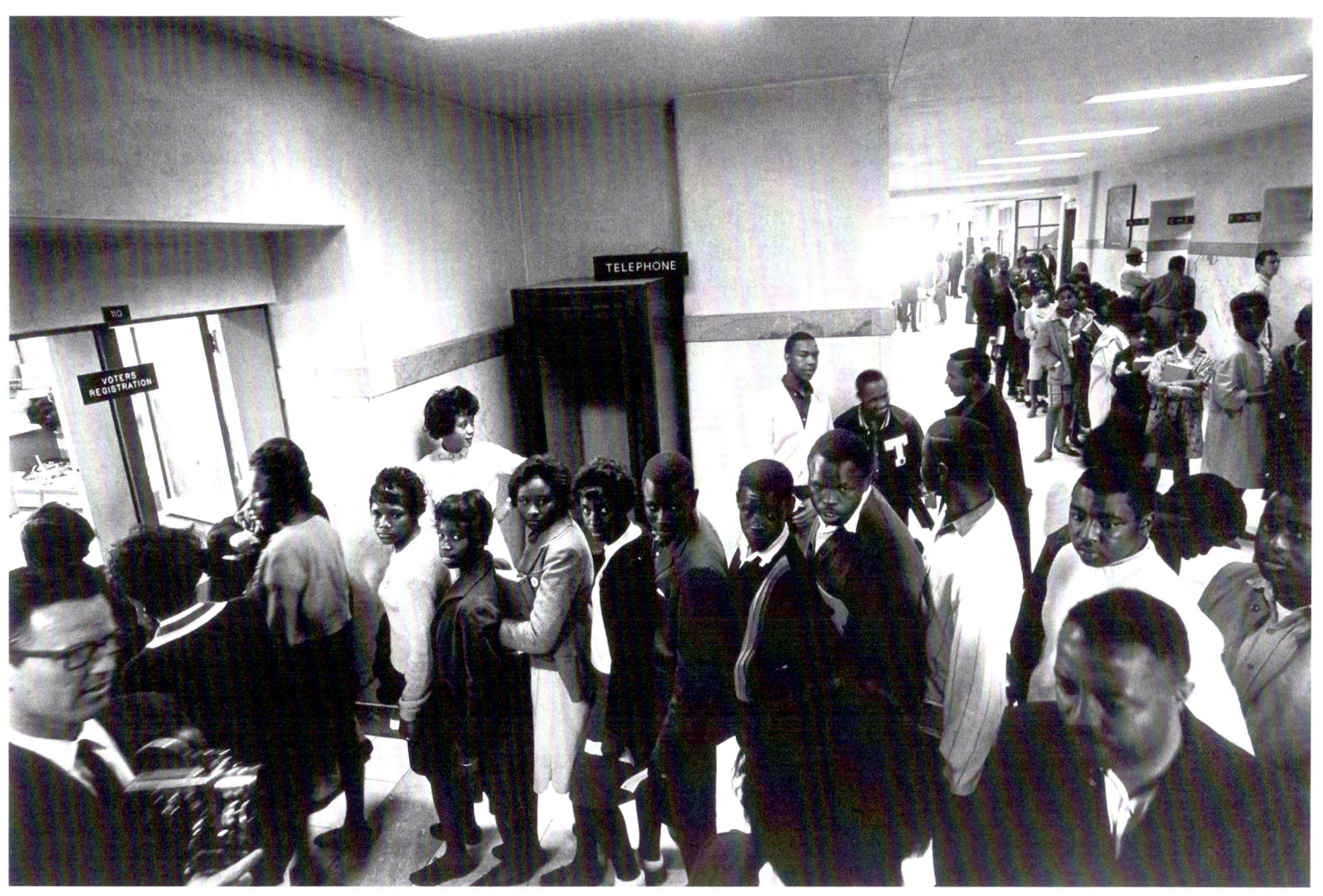

22. Voter Registration, Chatham County Courthouse

One night at the East Side Theatre—the place was packed—I was just covering it as a reporter that night.*…I remember it was one of Hosea's best talks, and I remember (him) standing up there and telling the people about the day he took his little boy by the hand and they walked by a restaurant, or drug store, soda fountain or something, and "my little boy said, 'Daddy, I want a hamburger.' And I said, 'Son, I can't take you in there to buy you a hamburger because they won't let black people in there. That's for white folks only.'" Of course, I'm not delivering it the way Hosea did, and man, you could just feel the tension in that place. The audience was kind of laid back and quiet, but the rumblings…you could see that he was recounting the experience of every black person in there.

—Archie Whitfield

I'll never forget arriving. It was dark when we arrived and there was a meeting going on at the time. We walked in and the place was jammed, by my memory at the time, I thought several hundred people. I walked in in the middle of a Benjamin Van Clark speech. Now that is an experience! Because Ben was rolling that evening and then Hosea got up. And to me, the most dramatic thing I saw that night, I saw it other nights, was the innovation that Hosea Williams and his friends voted to come up with was the nighttime demonstrations because a lot of people worked during the day.

…And to me the most interesting thing, and I'm reminded of it when I saw Gandhi a while back,…was the big basket being passed around and it was Hosea and Ben Van Clark and a couple of other people doing the exhortation. People, young men in particular, taking out knives, and switchblades, and zappers, and brass knuckles, all sorts of things being tossed in this bag so that when the demonstration began after the speeches, people would not have on them weapons so that if there were civil disobedience, that it could be said that none of the demonstrators had weapons on them. To me that was an incredible act, series of acts, of people being willing to participate and to buy into nonviolence.

And also some sets of individual with their knife or their blackjacks were willing to forego that individual—that reassuring instrument—in order that the group wouldn't look bad if there were a bunch of arrests.

And so this basket would just fill up. It was very interesting. This would go on night after night. It was a very interesting experience.

—Rick Tuttle

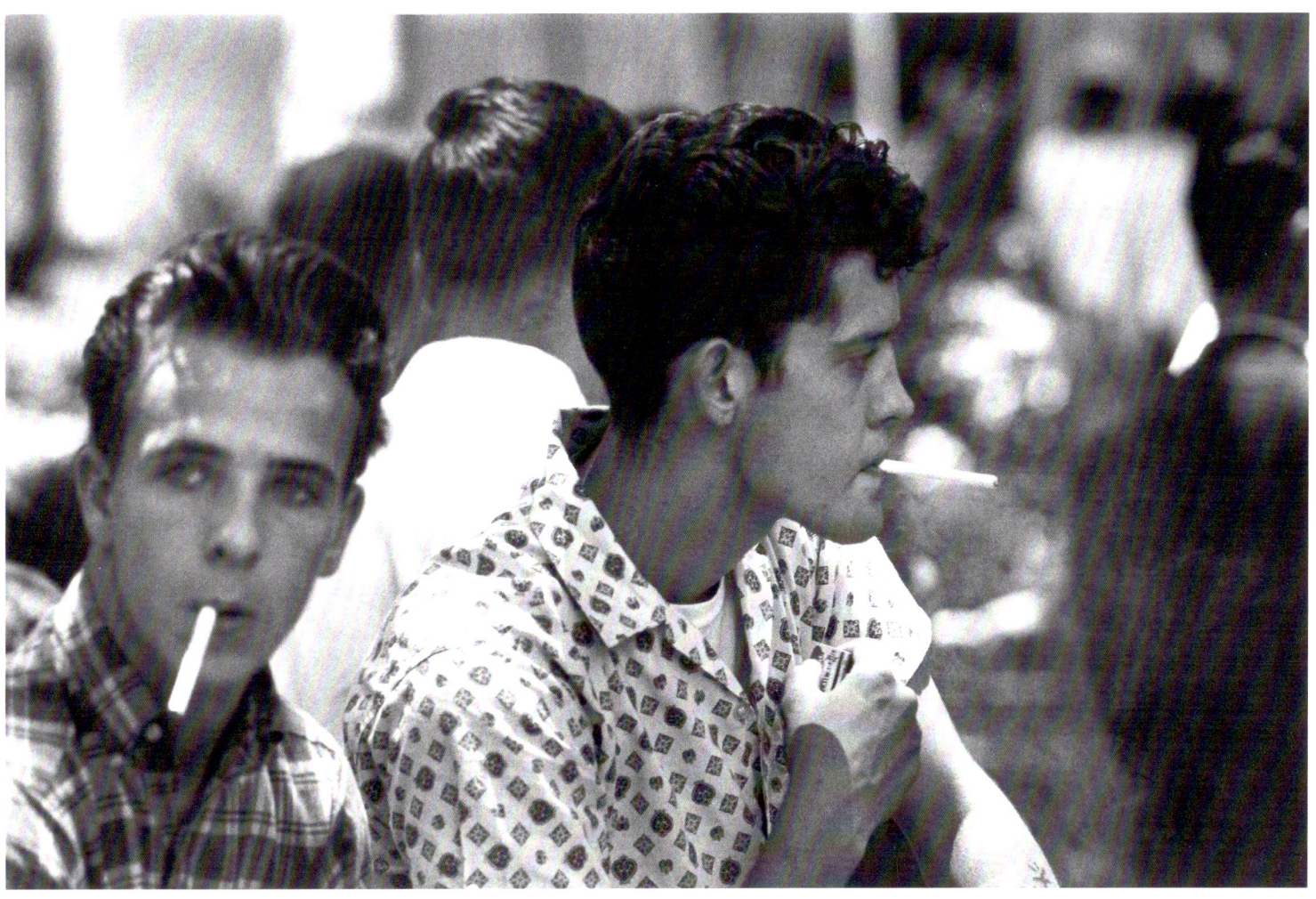

23. Taking a Drag, Wright Square

Sit-Ins, Day Marches, Night Marches

They had special groups that they felt wouldn't fight back because they didn't want no incidents like that. Ben Clark was the main one and Benjamin West. I can remember those two, 'cause they would never fight back, they would always go to jail....They were the type that could sit there and take that. I felt like I couldn't. And they went to Kress. I remember quite frankly, Ben West was spat upon and called everything, you know. Received a black eye and everything down there....Just sit there and take it. Well, I could never picture myself sitting there doing that.

—James W. German

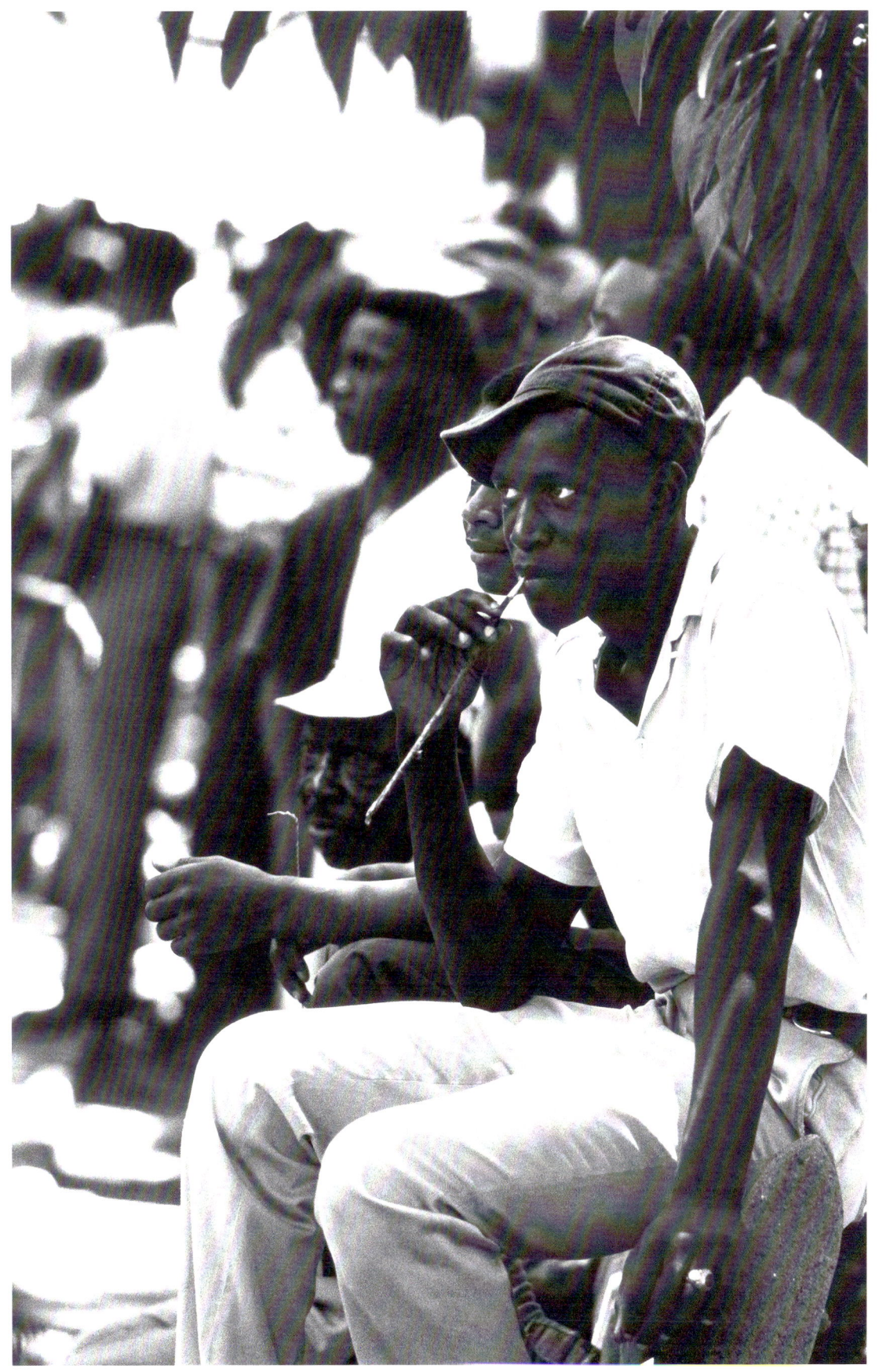

24. Listening, Wright Square

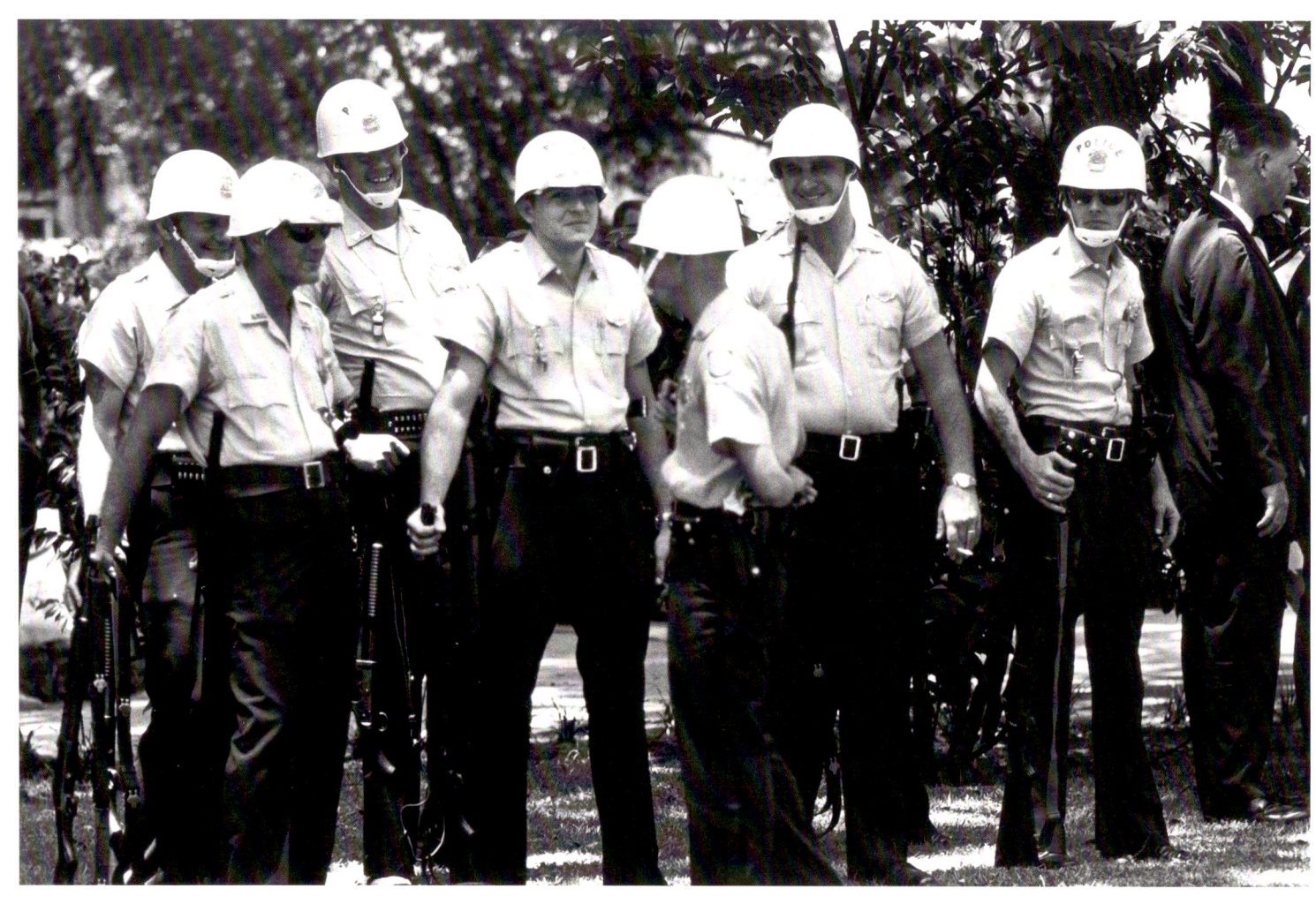

25. The Riot Squad

The polices treat the marchers alright. See, Mayor Maclean, he told them not to bother them. He told them to protect them. If they didn't protect them, why then they wouldn't have no job.

—James C. Middleton Sr.

Well, my position of course, I am sworn to uphold the laws, being a police officer. All of us are sworn. And about this time we had a law that was called the anti-trespass law, which, in effect, if a person came in your place of business, and you did not care to serve him for whatever reason, it didn't make no difference, for whatever reason, the owner of the place had to, in the presence of a law enforcement officer, he had to tell the person that he would not serve him or his group or multiple or what. He would not serve him and if he (the customer) refused to leave, he (the proprietor) would have no choice but to have him arrested. Consequently, they would say this in our presence, and if the person would refuse to leave then, we would have no choice but to tell him to (leave). Of course, we permitted them to call their lawyers.... It was all planned…very well in advance it was planned. In fact, Savannah probably was one of the proving grounds for the civil rights demonstration in the South because Hosea and Benjamin and Paxton and Willie Bolden and the rest of them exercised the, well this was the training ground.

—Sidney B. Barnes

One day I was downtown paying some bills, I stopped to listen to him (Hosea) and I liked what he was talking about. He was talking about Tomo-Chi-Chi—how they could put a rock there about him and the peoples had money for the poor to buy food but they wouldn't allow them to go in the places to buy it on account of their race and color. How they had the blacks cooking food, serving the food, but we're not good enough to sit down by them and eat. That's what woke me up then. I said, "Well, if we are cooking the food, and serve it to them, and we got money, then why can't we sit down by them?" I wondered about that. I said, "Well, I'd like to go sit down and buy me a steak and sit down and enjoy it." And, they refused to let us in there…. You couldn't get in Morrison's Cafeteria. They locked the doors on us. We just laid in front of the door. They had to tote me from in front of that door. I had money enough to buy five or six steaks…. I ended up going to jail that very day in front of that door. Me and four or five more of us, and I've been in the movement ever since.

—Lester "Big Lester" Hankerson

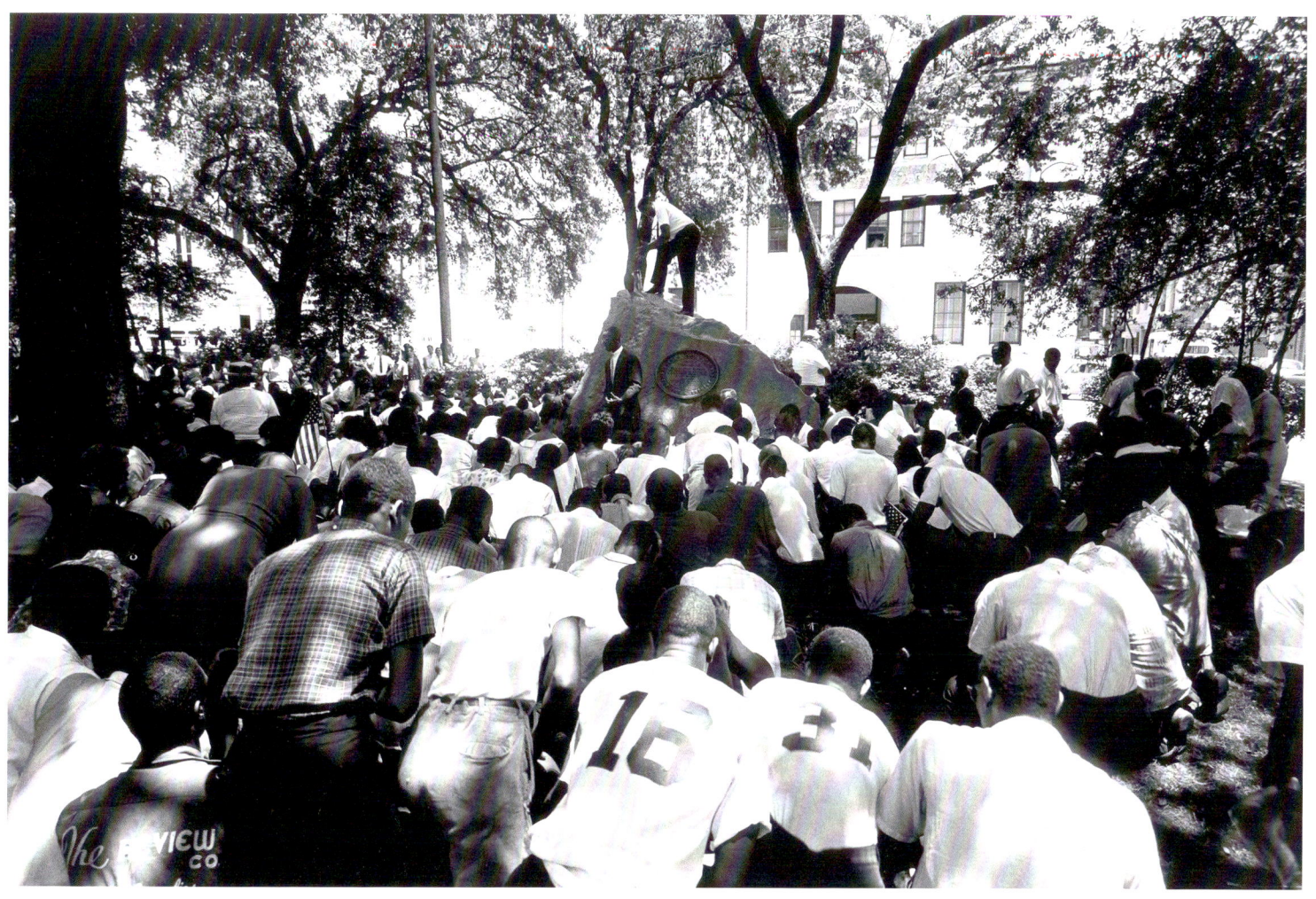

26. *Hosea Williams Preaching from Tomo-Chi-Chi's Rock*, Wright Square

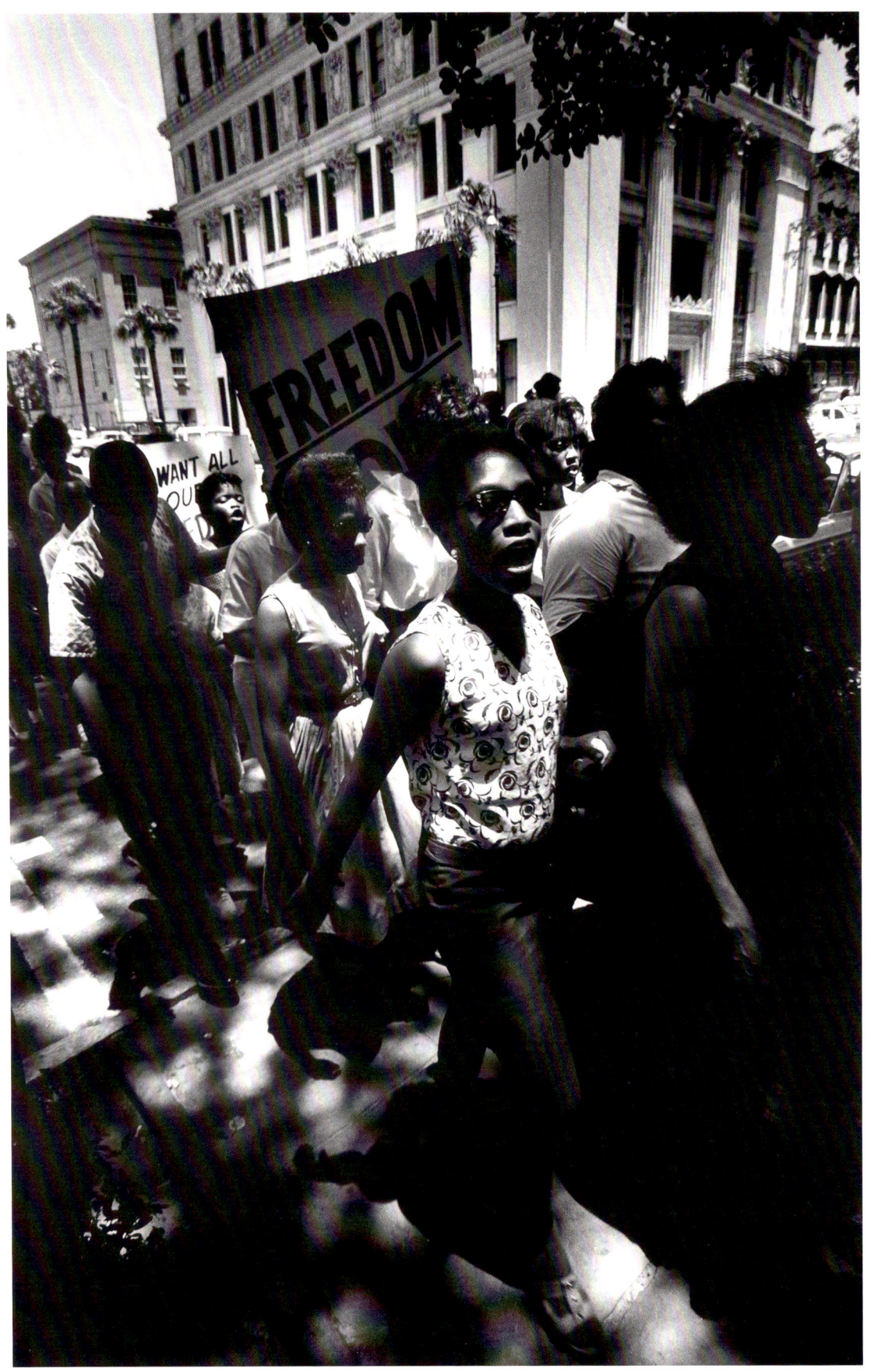

27. Singing Freedom Songs

Number one, it kept the people together. Singing helps to keep things organized. Because you have a kindred of spirits there, everyone on one accord.* (We sang) *Ain't Nobody Gonna Turn Us Around* and *We Shall Overcome*, which was the theme song. I used to write a few songs and make up the lines to various tunes.* One I wrote was put to the tune of *Michael Row the Boat* and we used to sing a lot of the old Negro spirituals. But our favorite, I think, was the theme song and *Ain't Gonna Let Nobody Turn Us Around*. That was a well-liked one, we liked that because it really got the spirit in us.*

—Carolyn Roberts Barlow

We, meaning the City, never attempted to stop black demonstrators from marching, though we did ask that they tell us where they were going to be and what their route was going to be so that we could ensure that necessary precautions would be taken to ensure that everybody would be protected. We did not want to have clashes between the blacks and the whites and we worked diligently to ensure that that would not happen. If necessary, we would, if there was a white group that wanted to demonstrate, we made sure that it stayed apart from the black group, but we didn't permit the two to come in contact with each other.

Then it grew larger. First there were daytime marches.* Then they began to have nighttime marches and I (the City Manager) was present at every march and the City Attorney was present at most of them with me. Our purpose was to ensure that the police did not overreact and that police exercised extreme care and caution to conduct themselves within the law. Whenever someone sat in, or whatever; we made it clear to the party (store owner) that he would have to bring charges. If he brought the charge, then the police made the arrest, but if he was not willing to bring the charge, we would do nothing. We did not ourselves initiate any arrests on private property at any time.*

—A.A. "Don" Mendonsa

We never really worried too much in the daytime because we felt that people could see…but at night it would be more terrible because you marched down the street where there ain't no lights, you know, and anybody who wanted to get even, could get even in the dark, you know.

—Benjamin Van Clark

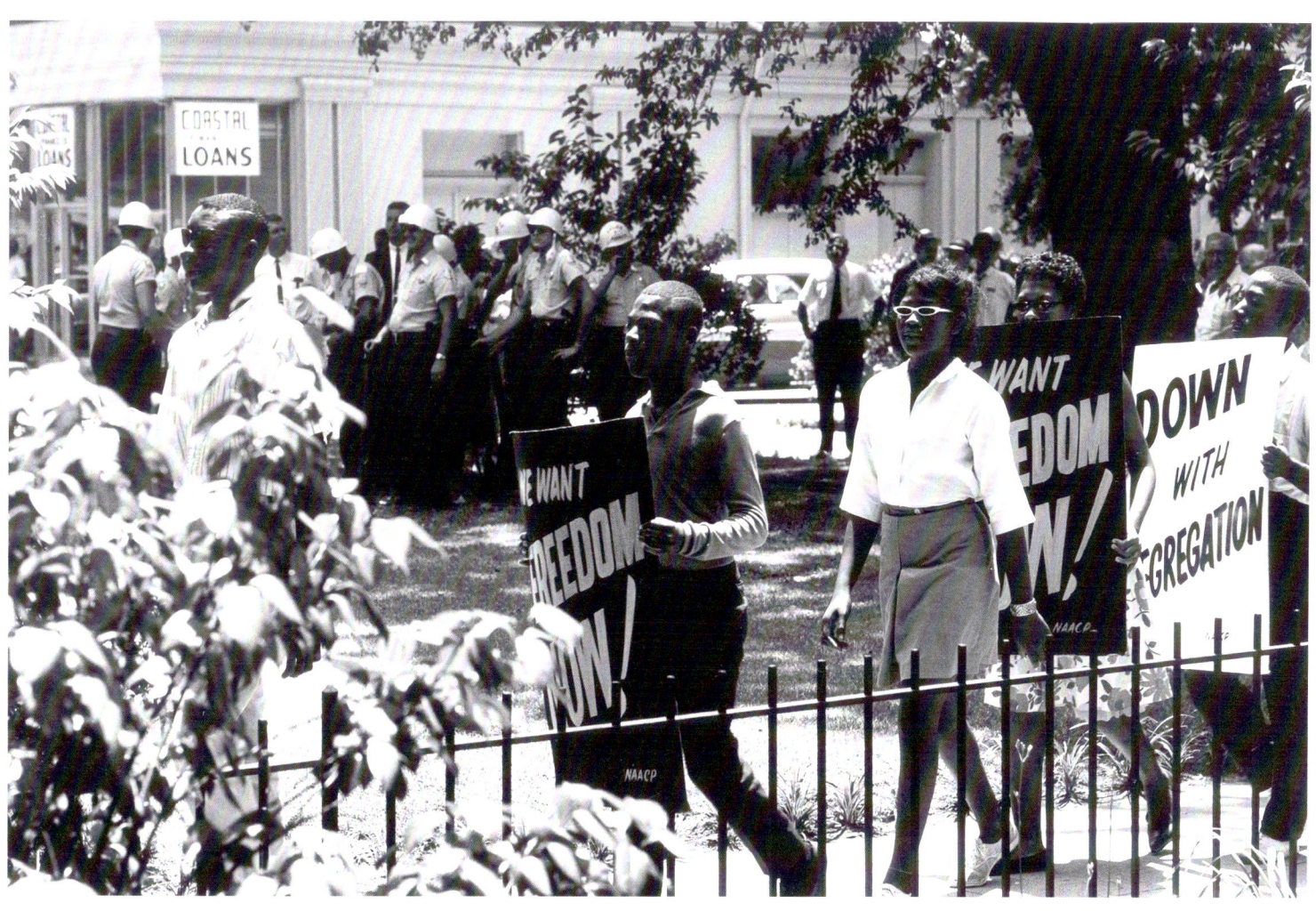

28. Marching for Freedom

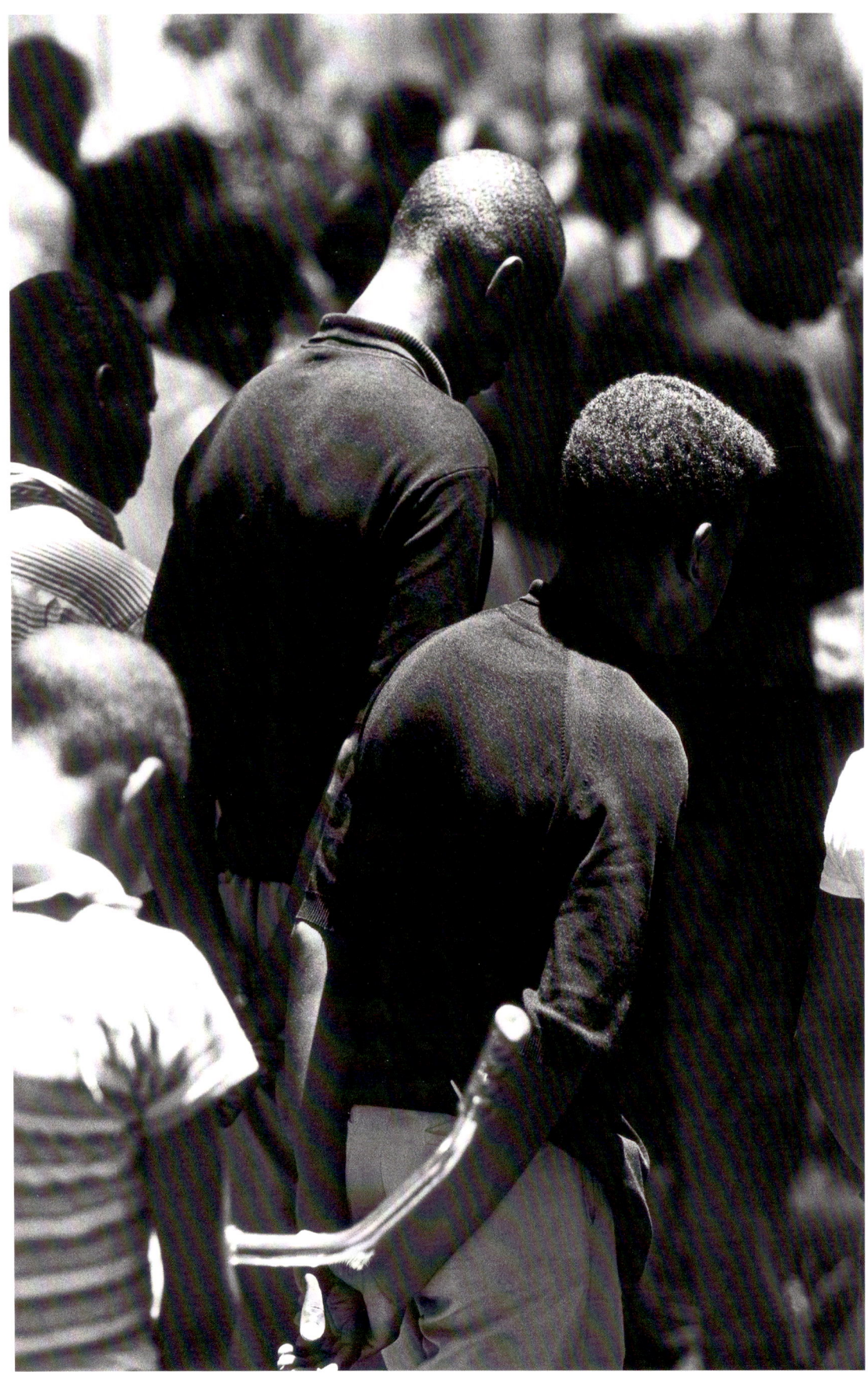

29. Prayer, Wright Square

I was willing to die, I know that. Many a night I thought I would die. Ummmm. You talk about a scared black man! And you listen to Hosea Williams you'd be willing to die. He would lead you anywhere.

—Henry "Trash" Brownlee

And then we had the riot down at the County jail. Well, the County police, to me, got a little overanxious and we were down helping them out with the crowd and what happened, the wind was blowing our way and we were the ones that got tear-gassed. And the ones they were gonna tear-gas didn't get tear-gassed. So, here's all the City police that were there helping them out were the ones that got tear-gassed.

—Lawrence E. Mahany

I don't know how it was, but we got through this thing with a lot less trauma. We had trauma. We had individuals who were beaten. They had mace thrown in their eyes and I've stayed up at the courthouse all night trying to put drops in their eyes and so forth. But, we didn't get the real trauma that they got in a lot of towns where individuals were continually beaten or shot and all that.*

—Henry M. Collier Jr.

Remember one night we were marching on Habersham Street towards the jail house and a white lady ran out of the house with a shotgun on State and Habersham, or something? Any rate, Albert Mack, and Ben Wesley, Carolyn, Hosea, myself, Big Lester, Trash Brownlee—we were trying to monitor the line because we had about 500 to 600 people. And all of the sudden, somebody said, "Look out!" This lady ran out of there and cocked that shotgun and said, "You niggers better get!!!!!"

—Benjamin Van Clark

*Where * appears interviewees elected to edit their own quotes.

Arrests and Jail

I used to get arrested twice in a day. That's right. I'd say, "Don't ya'll close the cell, I'll be back!"

—Henry "Trash" Brownlee

Hosea Williams had started something in Savannah—he and Ben Clark and Willie Bolden—they called and asked me to come down and do a speech. And, I went down and made a speech. And then they decided to have a march afterwards. Well, they had evidently already decided to have a march….I think they had been marching and nothing had been happening. We'd been marching downtown, having a little prayer, turn(ing) around and coming back.

For some reason, that night when they got downtown in front of the Holiday Inn, which is still there, the police came up with paddy wagons and said everybody's under arrest. And folk were just anxious to go to jail. See, I mean by that, in that day, going to jail was a kind of symbol of independence. It was a statement of manhood. It was throwing off the yoke of oppression. And so people just started running, getting in the paddy wagons. And I looked around and because, we, see, in Birmingham we had trained people, we had taken several months to organize, and when folk went to jail, they knew what they were doing. And I was not where they were being arrested, I was sort of on the other side of the street. And it suddenly dawned on me that all these kids were going to jail and there was no leadership with them inside the jail that knew what they were doing. So, I just went on and tapped the officer on the shoulder and said, you know, I need to go too. And so I got in the paddy wagon and went to jail.

—Andrew Young

They put me in jail. All right, for every peace bond I needed a piece of property (that) was completely free of debt. If peace bond was for $2,500, like they put me in jail the first day, it tickled me because it was $2,500. Means $5,000 (for) two bonds. My wife brought $5,000 worth of bonds down there and they said $7,500....And they had one black guy down there (who) had this kinda property. He's the kind of guy called a root man and he brought all these deeds down there and he was going to get me out and he would sit up there and talk with the judge. He had a stack of deeds, I mean two feet high to get me out. And he just asked the judge; said, just in passing, "Judge, how long you think my property be tied up?" The judge said, "If I have anything to do with it, the rest of my life." So he took his deeds and went home.

—Hosea L. Williams

Broad-based Support of the Civil Rights Movement

Some fine people. They said I did a job and I appreciated it and I thank God that I could have something to contribute to the movement. And a lot of people is just like that, they didn't give they body, but they give they soul, they give they money, you know, they give they property, like Sloppy Joe Bellinger....He give us, when the church shut they doors on us, he give us the Flamingo on Gwinnett Street. We had to go out there, in the club, and have mass meetings.

—Alfonzo "Big Al" Rivers

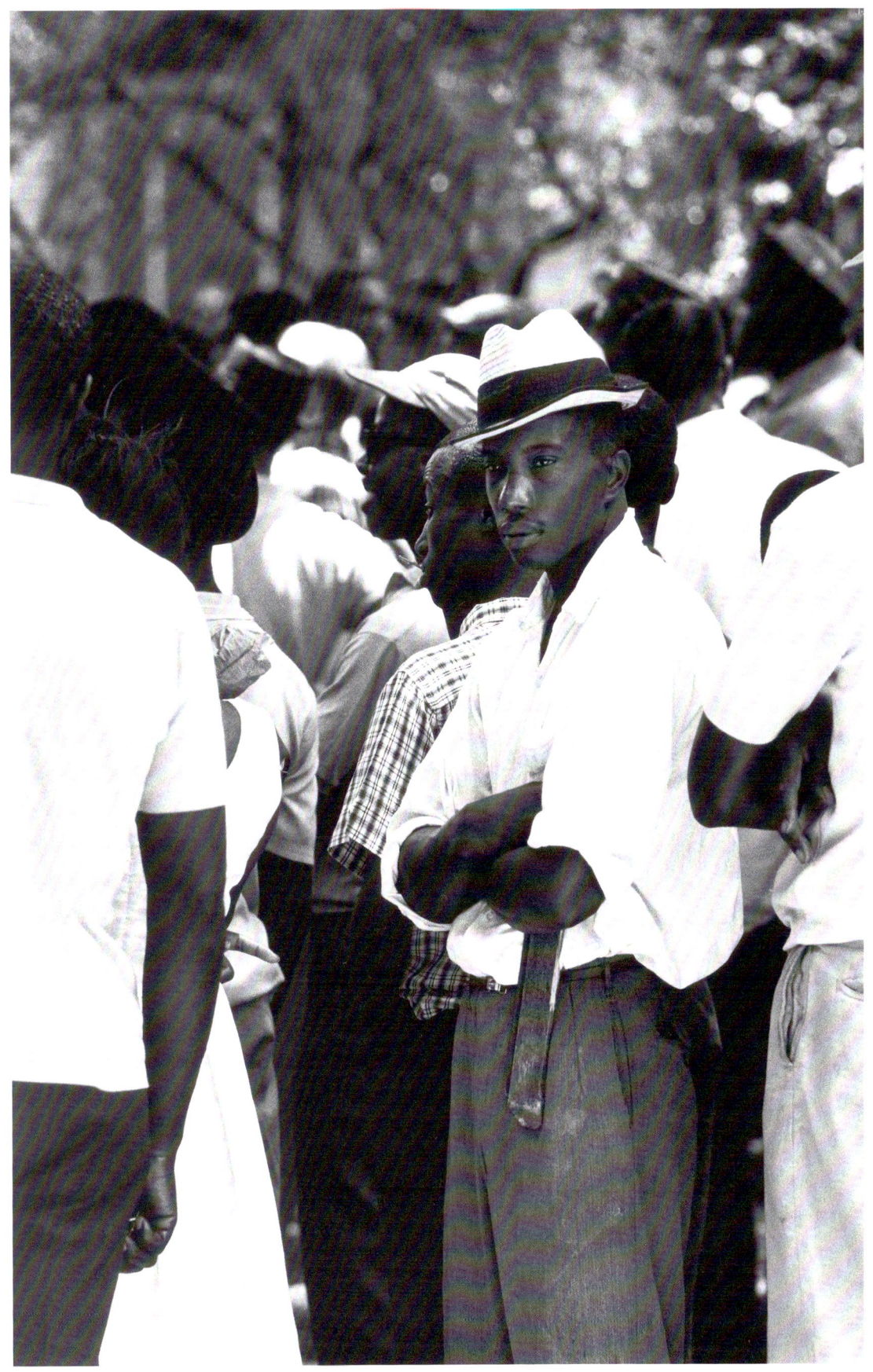

30. Onlooker, Wright Square

Even my mother, my mother didn't agree with me at all. But, I marched every afternoon, *every afternoon*. I passed out leaflets. I go to the mass meetings. I marched every afternoon from Gwinnet Street to wherever we was going to assemble. Every afternoon I was right there with them. …I felt like Ben was working for a good cause, and I was just so tired of going places and seeing a black go there and a white go there. If it was a bathroom—whatever you're going to the bathroom for—if this white lady's going in there, she's going to do the same thing I'm going to do but I couldn't go in the bathroom she was using.

A colored lady said one day, she thought that we were trying to do wrong to try to integrate these places, and we should stay in our place. It wasn't our place because the white folks was in front all the time and it wasn't our place to get out there and get into that. And, if she had that little whipper snapper called Ben, we were on the bus, and if she had that little whipper snapper, what she would to him. So she was going further than I was, and I rang the bell in time to get off, I said, "Well, ma'am, I'm sorry to say that, but that young man that you was speaking about, whipper snapper, that was my son." And I stepped off the bus.

—Rosalee Clark

There was old people, too old to march, but they put nickels and dimes on the table and fares and everything else. Oh yea, they housed all the kids who came from the north. They give them free room and board in the slums and stuff.

—Henry "Trash" Brownlee

The story have not been told. (There's) a lot of people want to stay in the background. (We) had a lot of whites that were 100 percent with us. A guy who had a grocery store, when we got from marches he had 80 to 90 pounds of meat and bread to serve us.

—Alfonzo "Big Al" Rivers

The black middle class were more conservative. They had come up under the old regime and they were timorous to start with. They all had the feeling (that) they wanted these things to happen, but there was a whole lot of problem about how it would happen and they felt that some of the black folk were too militant, so they held back. By and large, the black middle class did very little as far as the leadership was concerned. But when it came to supporting it with money and their property, they were willing to do that. We couldn't have done it without them because the people in the streets had nothing. And when it came to bonding out 300 people, or however, I guess it was more than that, we never would have made it if they hadn't come through. They wanted to do, but they didn't want to be in front. They had their friendships with the white community and they were to some extent afraid. They had more to lose, that kind of thing. Their jobs, at one time they began to try to intimidate people through the loss of jobs, the school teachers and people like that, so they were in the background helping, but not in the leadership. As things developed, as time went on, the middle class began to take on more of a leadership role when they saw that they had achieved some degree of freedom, it wasn't as bad as they thought it was going to be….Segregation was a terrible thing and these people had experienced it all their lives and they wished that it was not like that. But they always wondered what the consequences would be, but the kids didn't think about consequences, they just went on and did it. So it was a mix and I think everybody was glad when goals began to be achieved.

—Eugene H. Gadsden

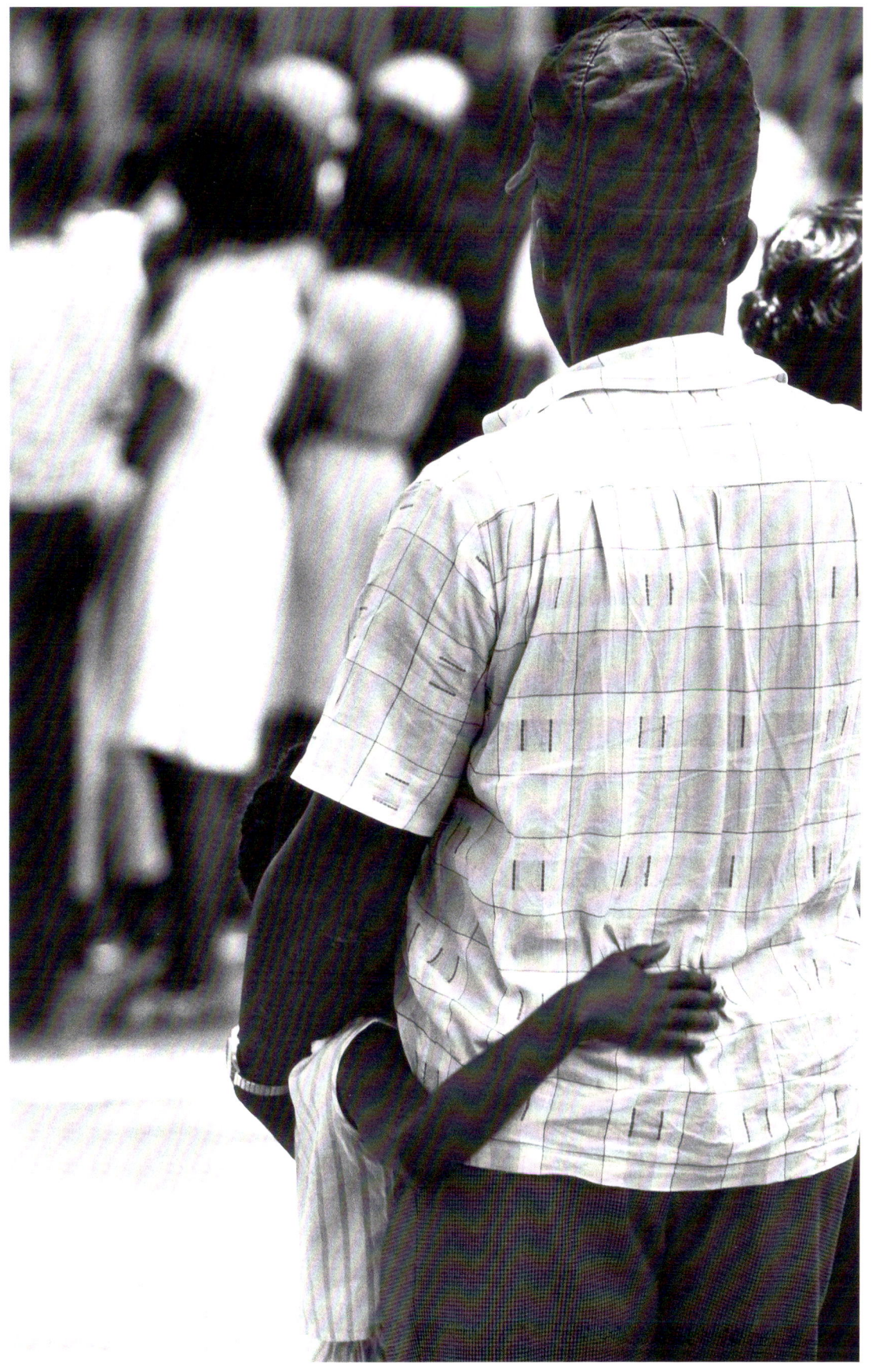

31. Father and Child, Wright Square

The Countermovement

I mean I had those kinds of experiences even as Ambassador at the Waldorf. I mean, I was the U.S. Ambassador to the U.N. and had a suite on the 42nd floor of the Waldorf Towers, and walking through the parking lot of the Waldorf and some big gentleman from Texas just, looks, but doesn't look, see, just sees somebody black, hands me his keys to park the car. You know, and you never get, you never get away from it. I took the keys and handed it to the fellow who was supposed to park the car. I said, "I think this is his responsibility." And he got embarrassed after he realized who I was. But, it happened.

—Andrew Young

The Klan were in abundance (at a rally in Forsyth Park). They were in their robes, and when I finished (speaking), one fellow jumped up on the flatbed of the truck and yelled "traitor" because I guess he thought that I was going to flame the crowd and (say) let's go march on the blacks. And they had him off (I guess it was the police) and they surrounded me and took me away.

Most people were there because they didn't know what to do. They couldn't get the truth from any element and they didn't know what was going on. Many of them felt, everything is being given to the blacks, they're losing everything. They just could see everything they'd worked for…they just felt like they were losing freedoms and everything.

I kept saying, that is not what is happening…I tried to work with them from there….

It was a very difficult time, I'm not sure I'd put my family through it again. My girls were small and they were threatened, cursed you know—telephone, you know, it was just a very bad time, because no one understood what anyone else was doing.

—Cecil A. Hodges

My name had appeared in the paper as John E. Cay Jr., which is my name, but I'm known as Jack. I walked in the house and Barbara says there is a phone call for you. This voice said, "Are you John Cay?" I said, "Yes, to whom am I speaking?" He said, "Well, I don't know who you're speaking to, that ain't important, but I know I'm speaking to a nigger lovin' son of a bitch" and hung up the phone.

I never gave it much of a thought, but I went to (my)…club the next day. (There)…was one of my best friends (whose)…company was one of our top accounts. So I walked in and sat down and had lunch with the boys and told them this as an amusing anecdote. I said some guy called and called me a "nigger loving son of a bitch." (My friend) said, "Yeah, and he's right, too." We didn't lose that account, but that's how the feeling ran back then.

—John E. Cay Jr.

Keys to Success

It was a strange thing, though, the people who were most adamant to begin with finally got to be our friends, you know. I think it really created a unique relationship between the races in Savannah. These people are dying out now so I don't know what the situation is among the young group of people, but I know in the past 10 years there wasn't any subject we couldn't discuss with people on a one to one basis. We didn't always agree, but we always could talk about it.

—Eugene H. Gadsden

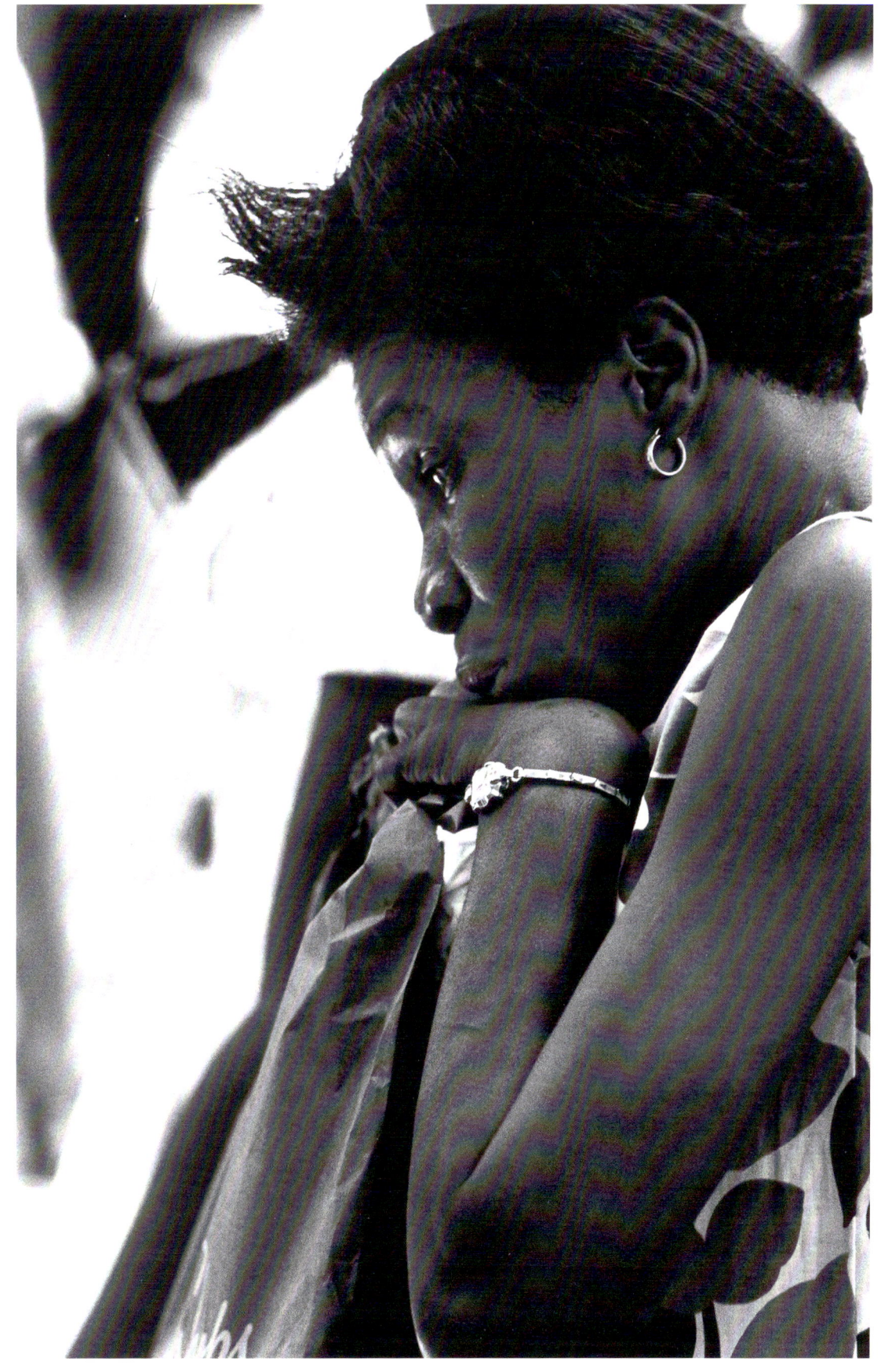

32. Thinking

The Committee of 100 and the Toomey Committee was almost one in the same. The Toomey Committee was a smaller version of it, but this was—in some other places in the south, committees of 100 were being formed and these were business people—supposed to be 100 business people to give leadership, you know to make the change and so forth.... It gave leadership and it gave us a place to come and do something other than demonstrate, because we could come and sit with people who could made decisions. And that's where we met Pratt Adams and people like that who were willing to listen. And Goldberg, who had been first to arrest the students, was a leader in trying to get the problems solved, because the boycott had really hurt.

—Curtis Cooper

It was a long summer. If I went to lunch, I had to always let the police know where I was. I would be at lunch and they would say, "They are marching and they're in Johnson Square," and then I'd come back there. At night they would march and we would be on the street until 2 o'clock and 3 o'clock in the morning. And I would go home and the phone would ring and it would be abusive calls and it would be continuous, so we'd take the phone off the hook in the kitchen so we could sleep. This went on for two or three months.

While the marching was going on, the Blue Ribbon Committee was meeting trying to resolve the conflict between the private business and the black demonstrators. Agreements were reached, but the blacks still had a group that wanted to march. They were to meet at a place called the Flamingo Club on Gwinnett Street. The leader of this group said to us, and this was understood, "We're going to march and you meet us and you stop us and you tell us you can't march tonight and we'll stop and say a prayer and then we'll go back." And that's what they did. We met them about where the little service station that still stands just west of the Gwinnett Street underpass (I-16). I walked up to them and said, "Okay now you'll have to stop, you can't march any more tonight." So they stopped. They stopped and they kneeled and prayed and then they turned around and went back and that was it. That was the last incident we had.*

—A.A. "Don" Mendonsa

But one of the things which popped out also was the fact (that) with the demonstrators… being dedicated to nonviolence, there was no expression or proclivity on the part of the other side to at least, in any large scale way, want to use violence to respond. I mean it was a very disarming, mutually disarming approach. And had it been otherwise, I think we could have had serious trouble throughout our country.

—Rick Tuttle

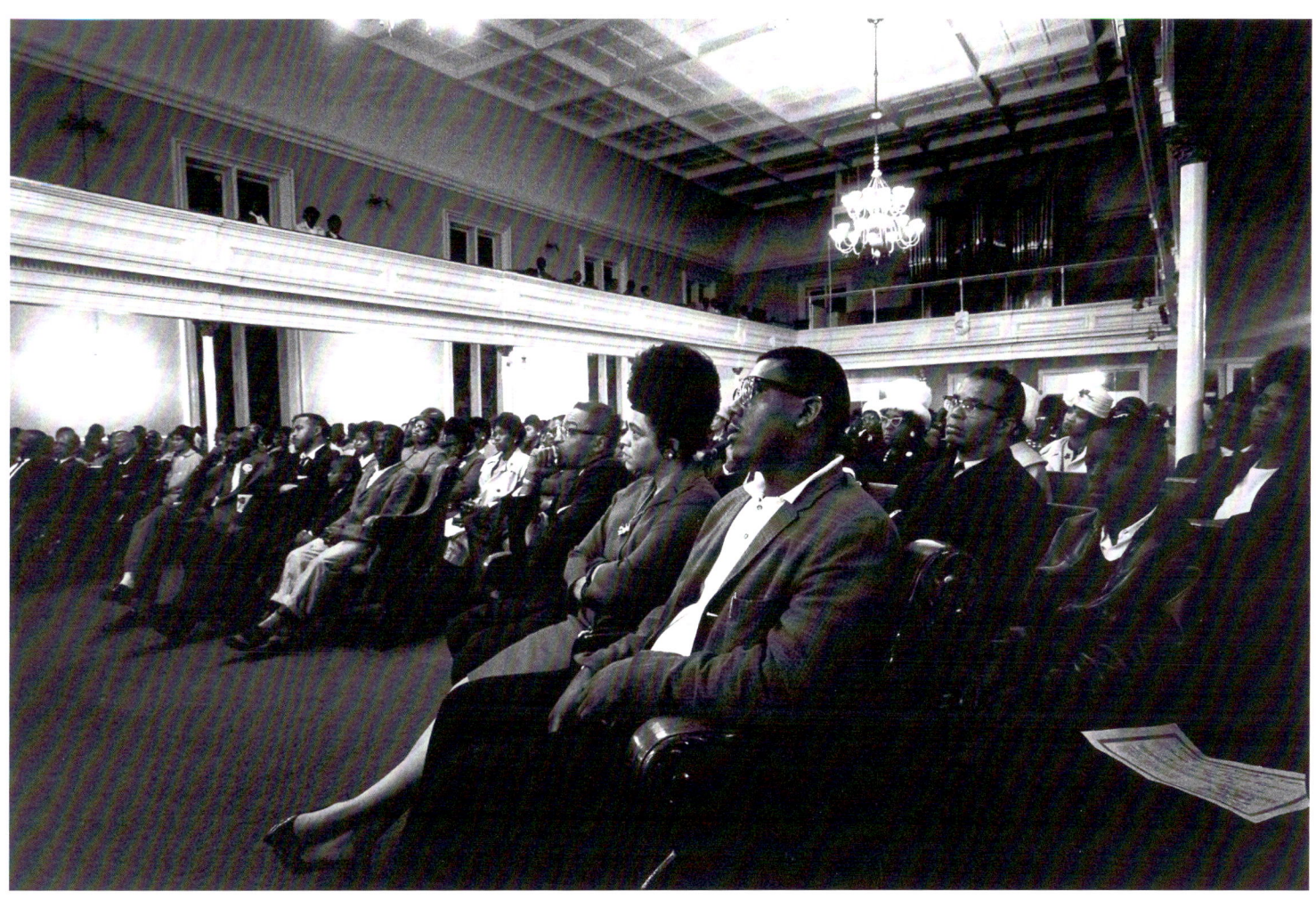

33. Audience, First African Baptist Church

Perhaps the most significant thing about our situation was that we, throughout the entire summer and throughout all the various things that happened, we never lost communication with the various principals or parties involved. The actors in the thing maintained some degree of communication throughout.

—James B. Blackburn

We weren't interested in burning the town down. We were interested in getting some rights. That's what we wanted to do. We loved Savannah. We love it now, and we didn't want to see anything destroyed. That's the other side of that question. What we wanted to be able to do was enjoy it like everybody else was enjoying it. Use the squares and do all that....

—Curtis Cooper

Epilogue: Dr. King

Who wasn't there? It was a perfectly marvelous experience. I'm telling you, his charisma was something. When he came down that aisle, it was just like Jesus Christ had walked into the auditorium! That's right, and he was a spell binder. Oh, it was just a marvelous experience, marvelous experience.

—Martha W. Wilson

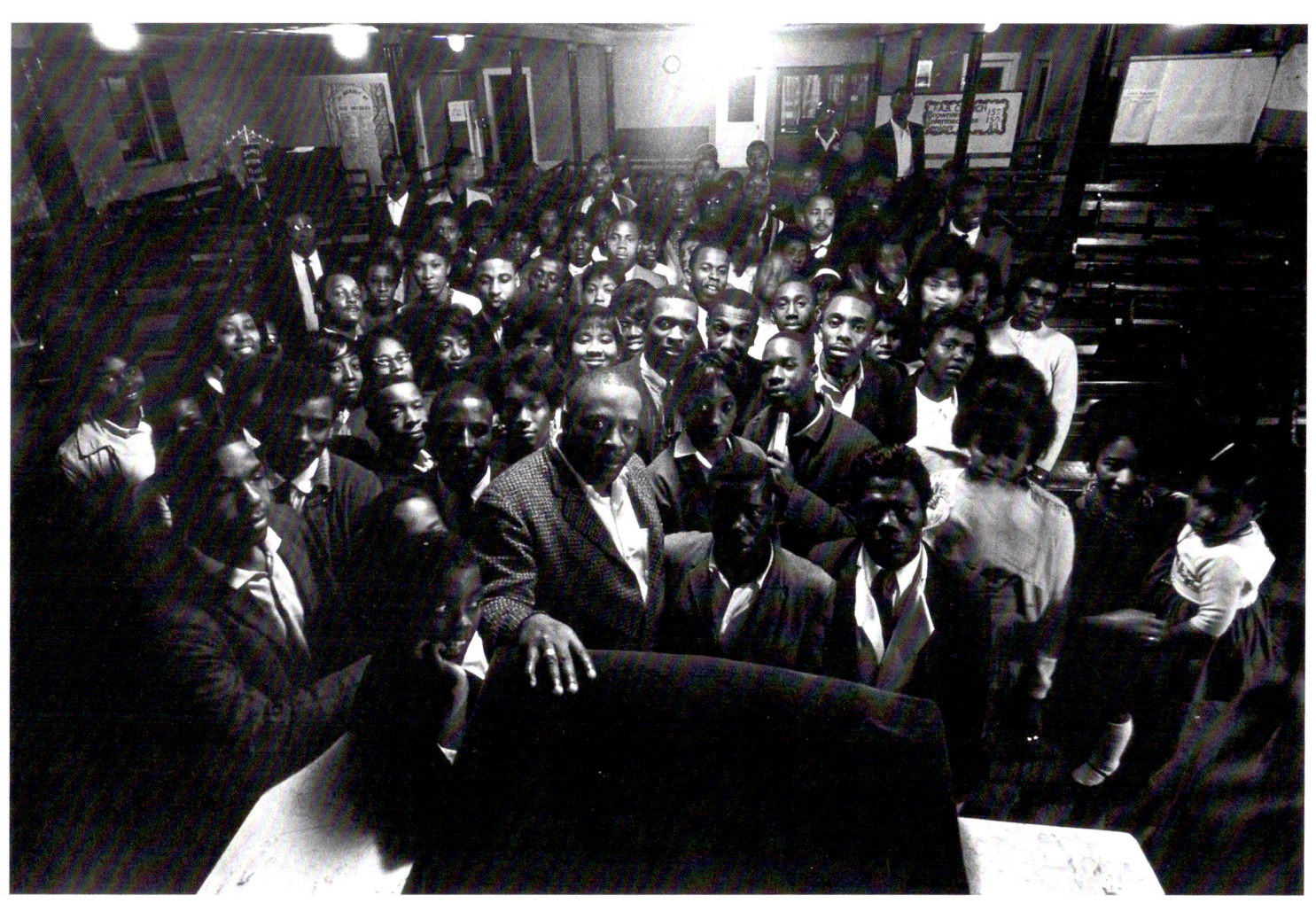

34. Anticipation, First African Baptist Church

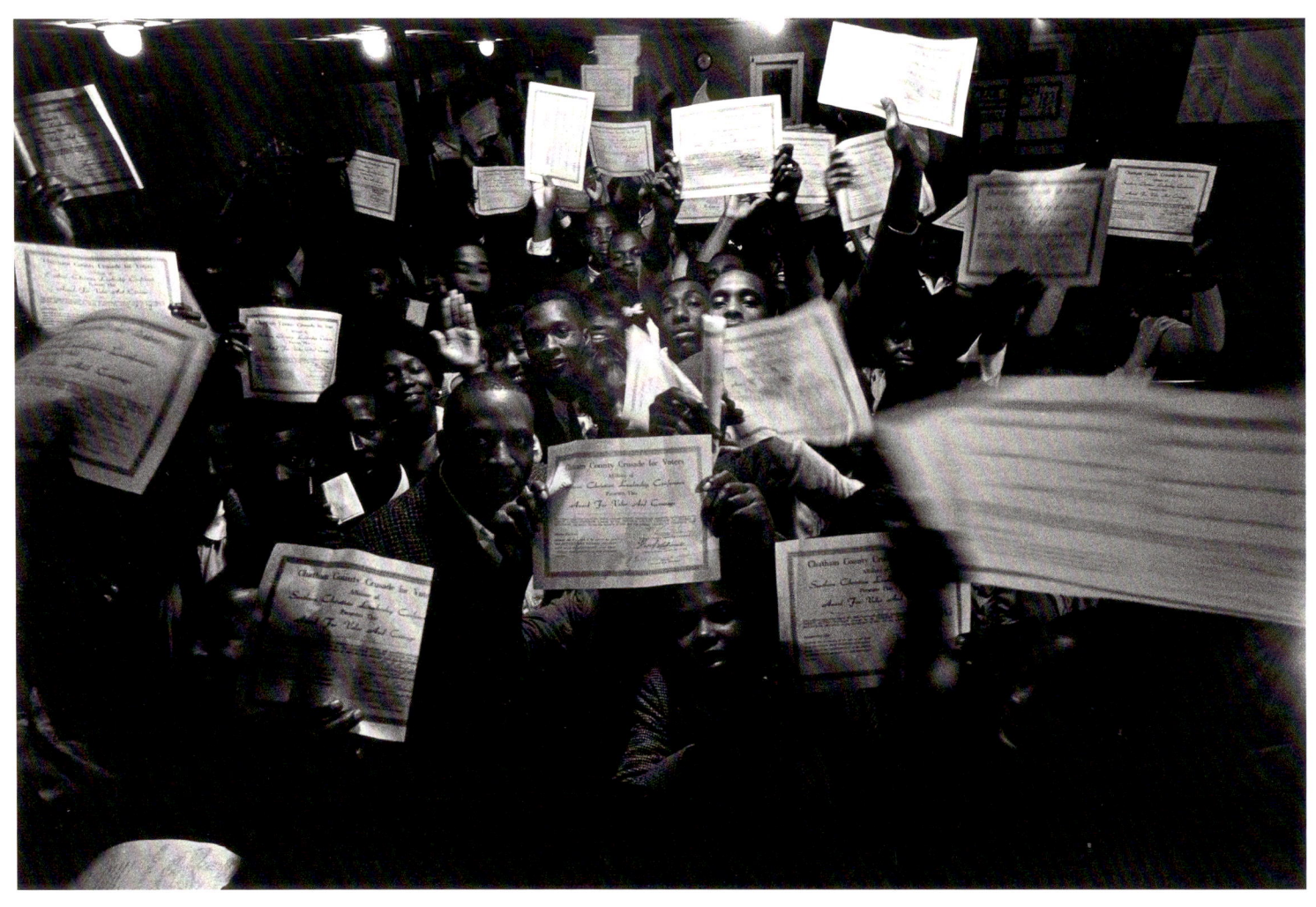

35. Waving Certificates of Courage, First African Baptist Church Basement

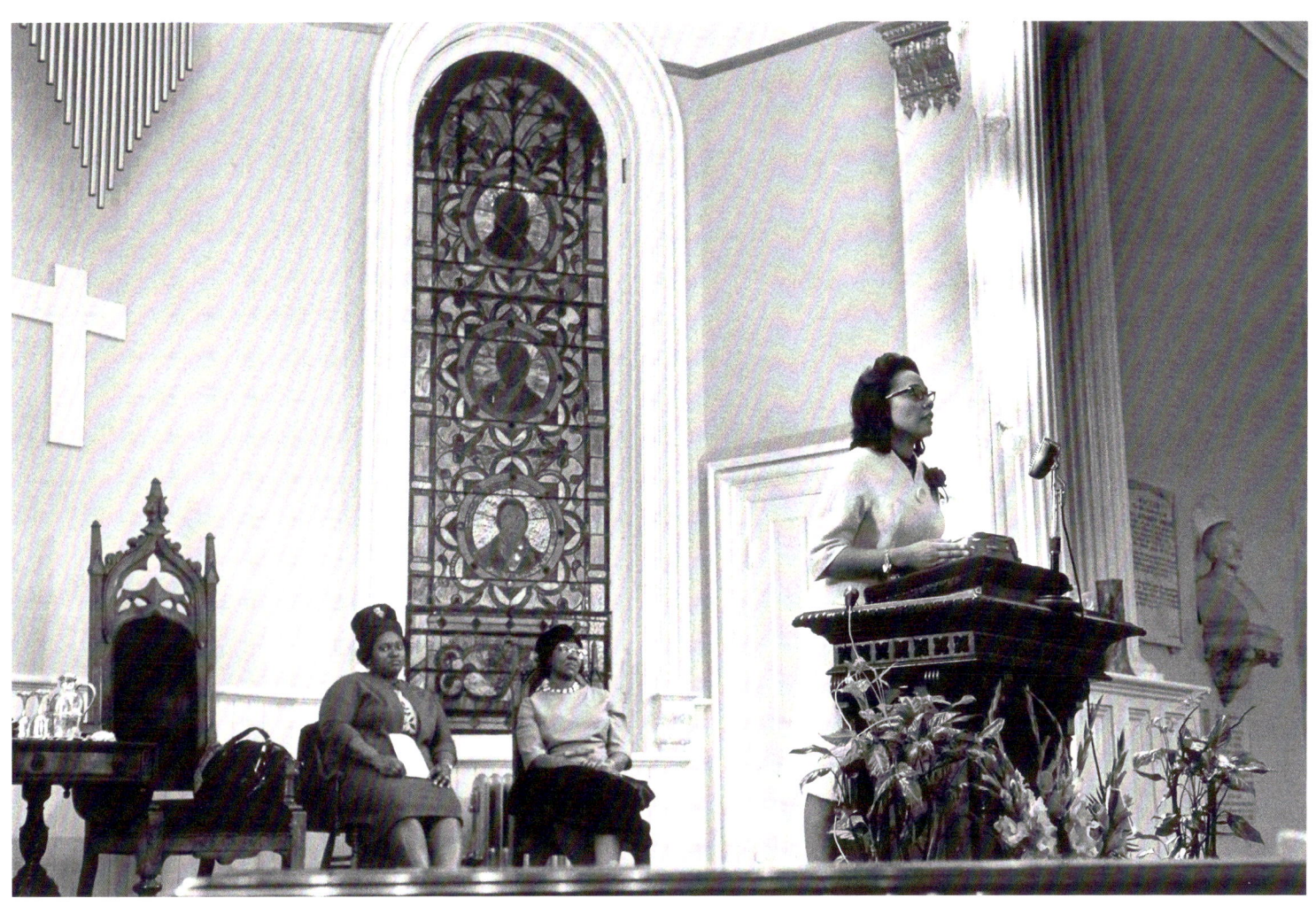

36. Mrs. King, First African Baptist Church

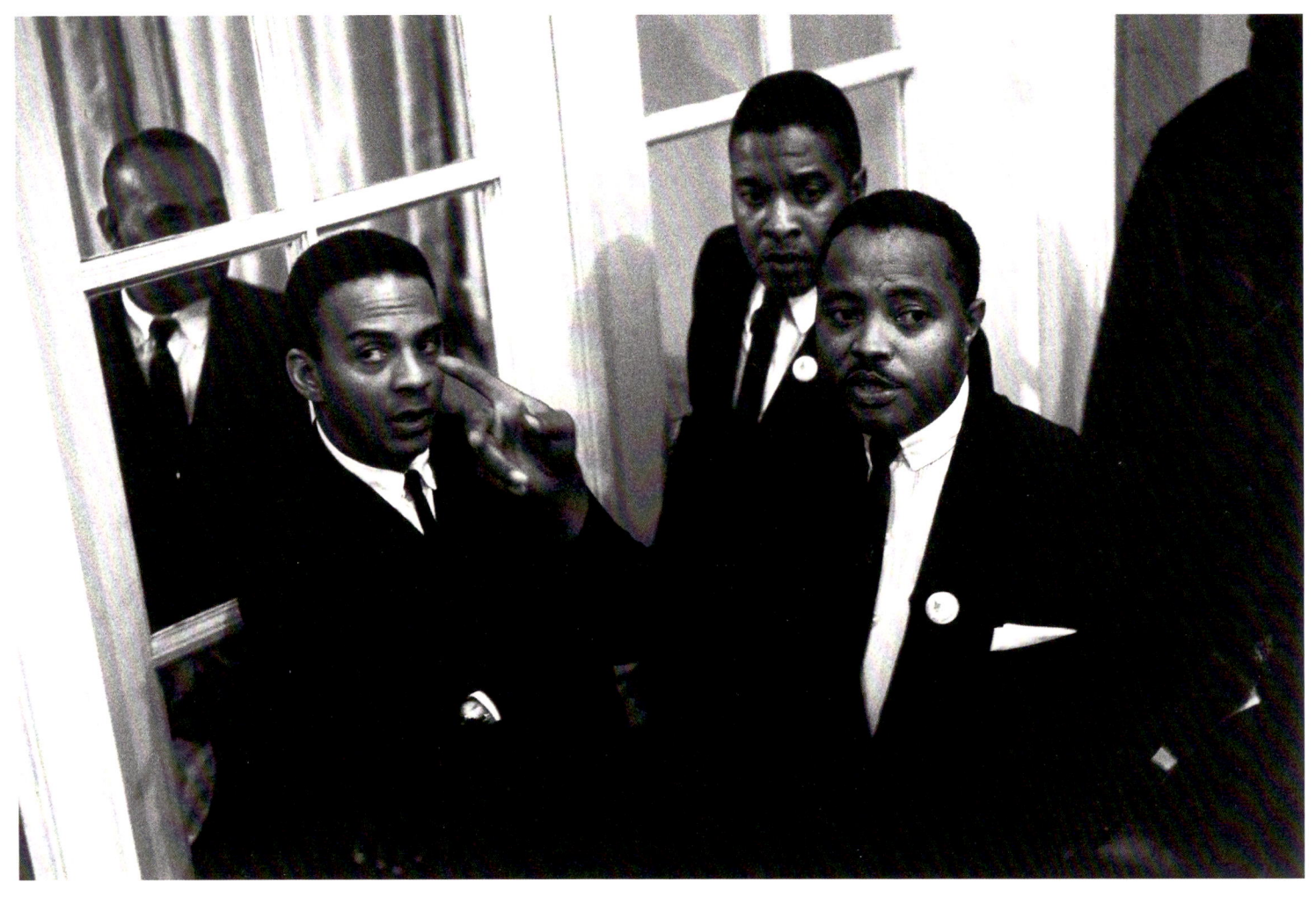

37. Andrew Young, Hosea Williams and B. Clarence Mayfield Waiting for Dr. King, Municipal Auditorium

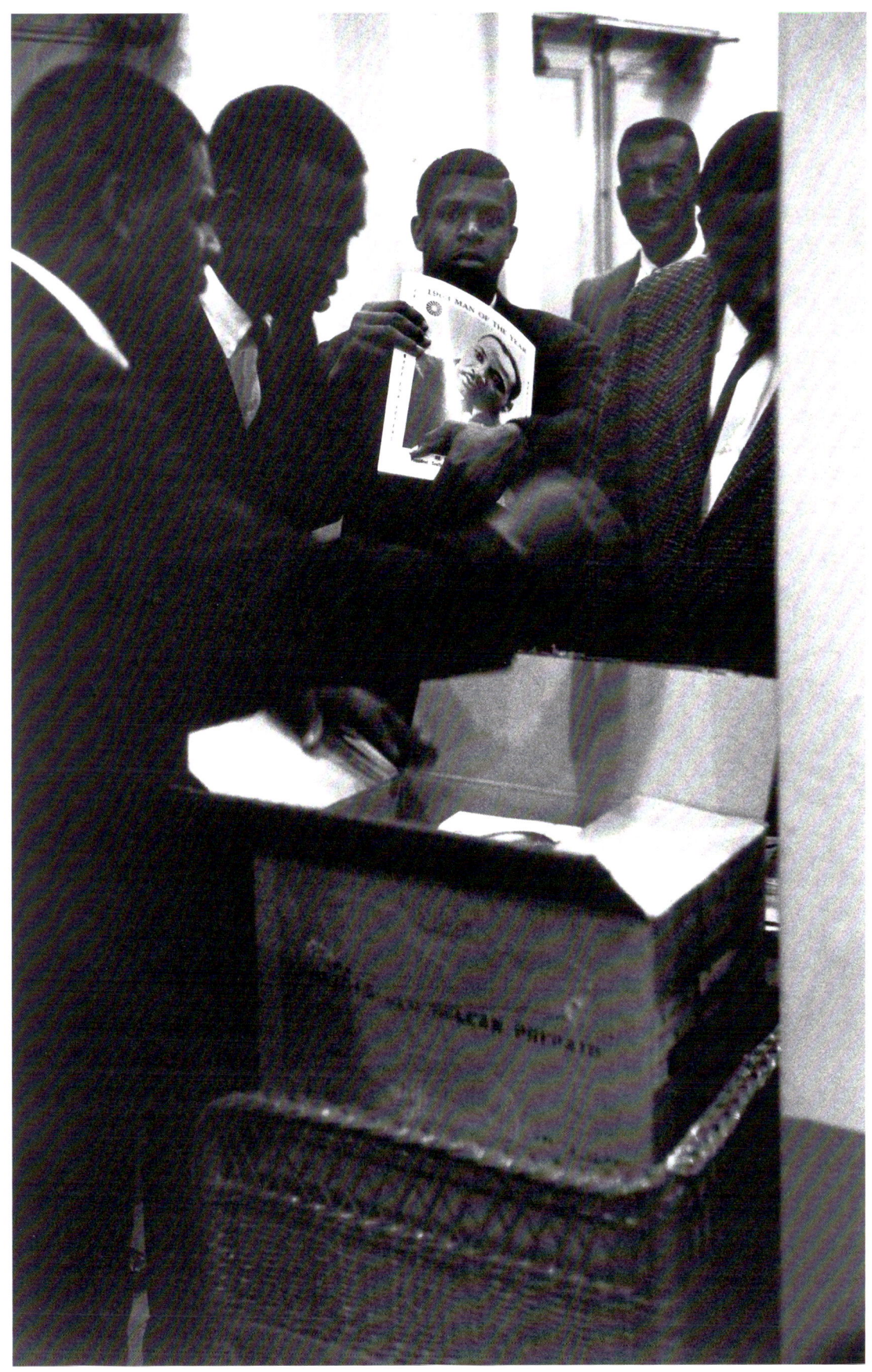

38. Unpacking Handbills

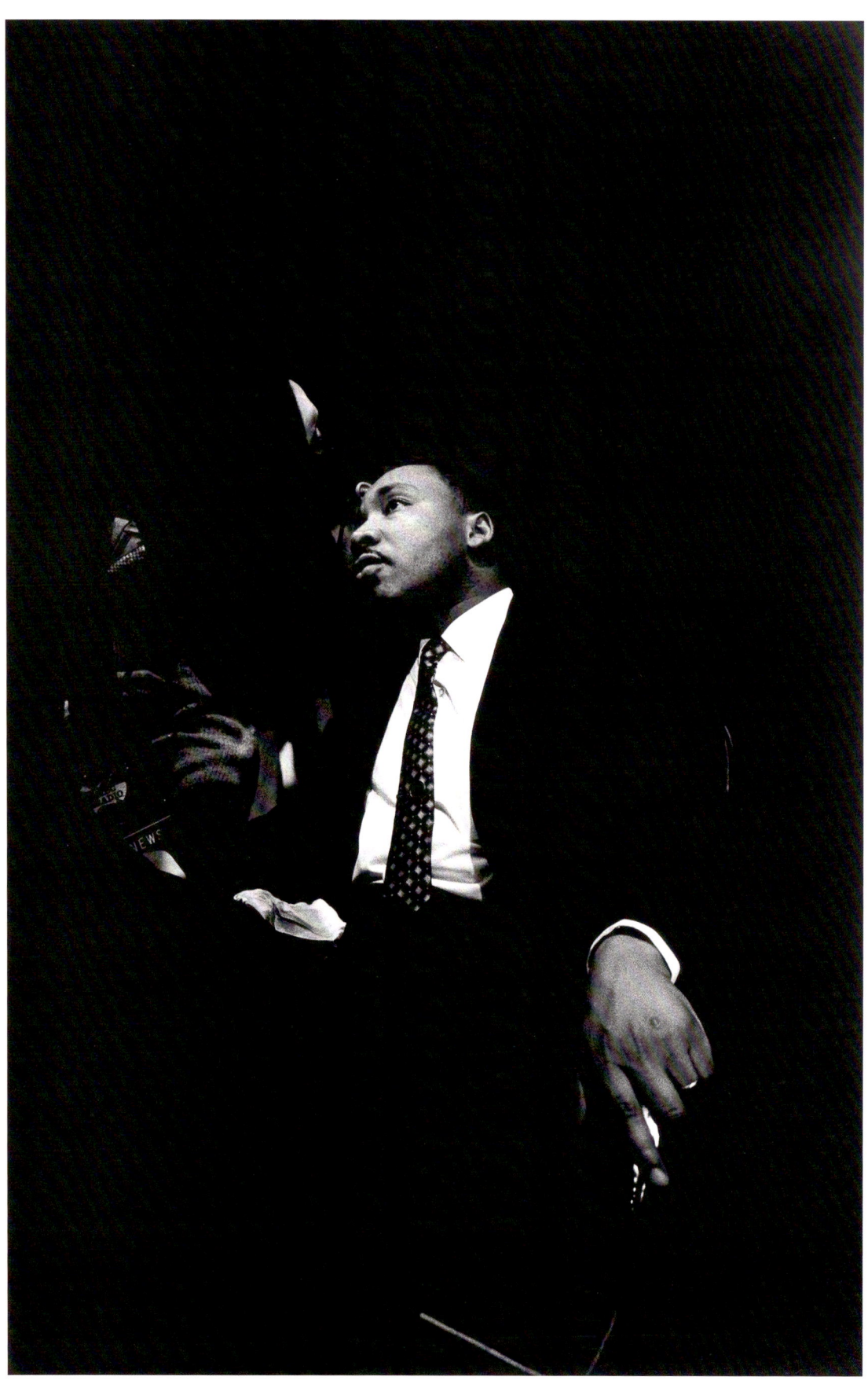

39. Press Conference, Municipal Auditorium

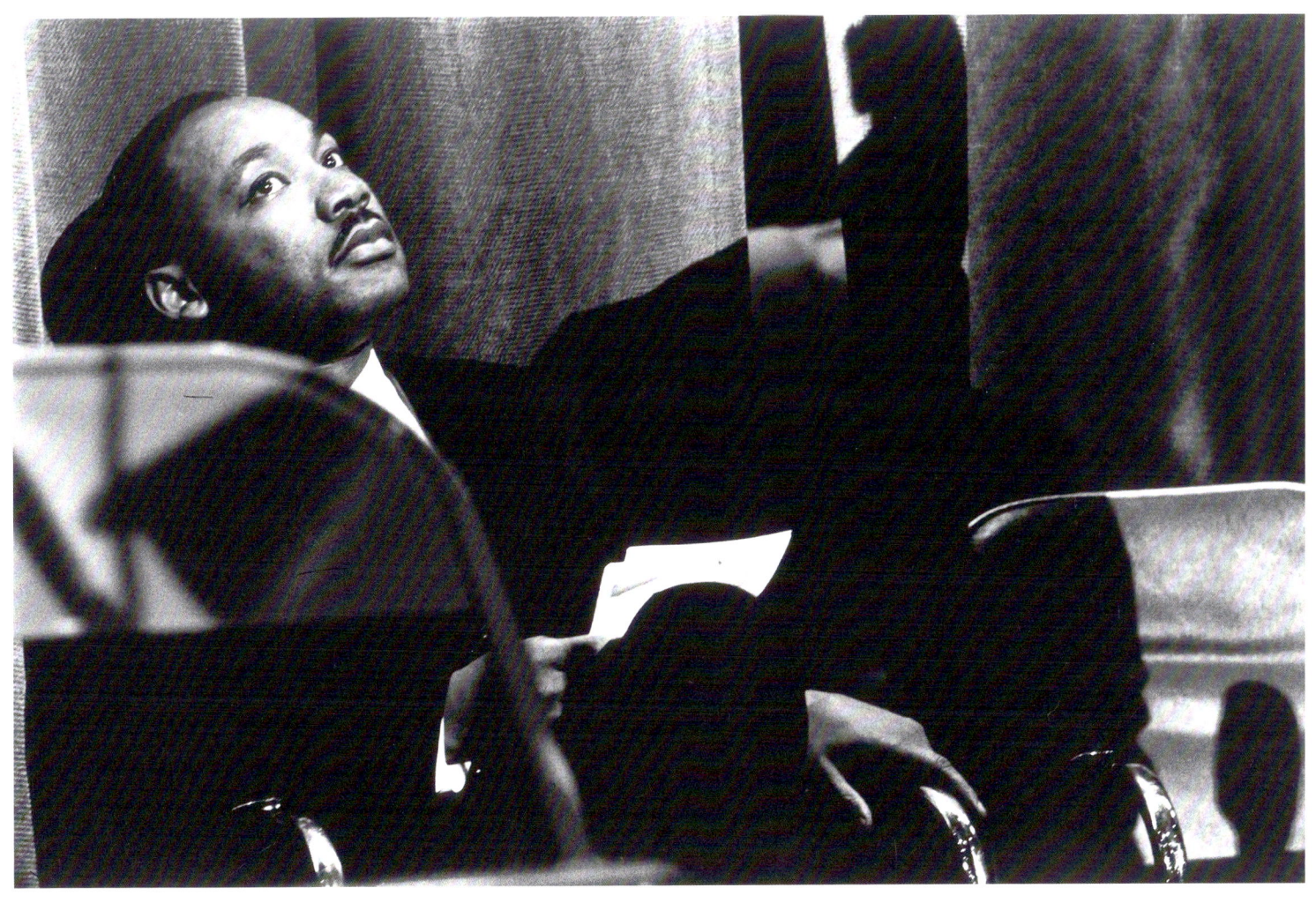

40. A Moment of Relaxation, Municipal Auditorium

On the platform he was, I don't know how to describe his oratory, but it seemed to be rhythmic. But when he sat on the porch, he was just talking. He talked like a black boy to us. And he used terms like "man" and "that cat" and that kind of stuff, you know. But you could tell that he was a guy of great depth and vision, even then. But he put us all at ease and we could ask him questions and that kind of stuff. So that was a great moment.

…You know I think he eventually discovered that he was somebody special. But I don't believe that when he came to Savannah he really knew how special he was. He certainly didn't act like that. I mean, really, you wouldn't believe it.

—Curtis Cooper

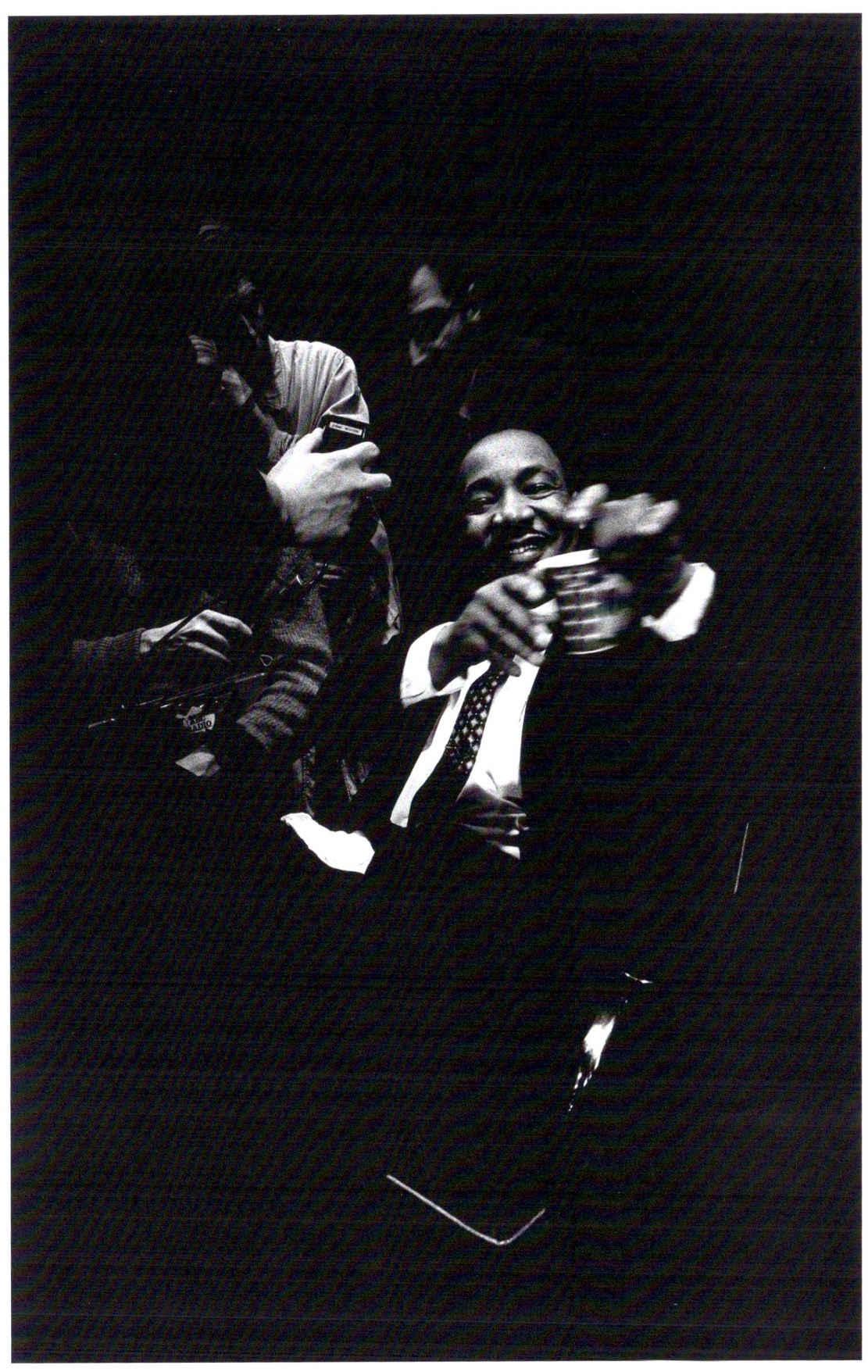

41. Sharing a Joke with the Press, Municipal Auditorium

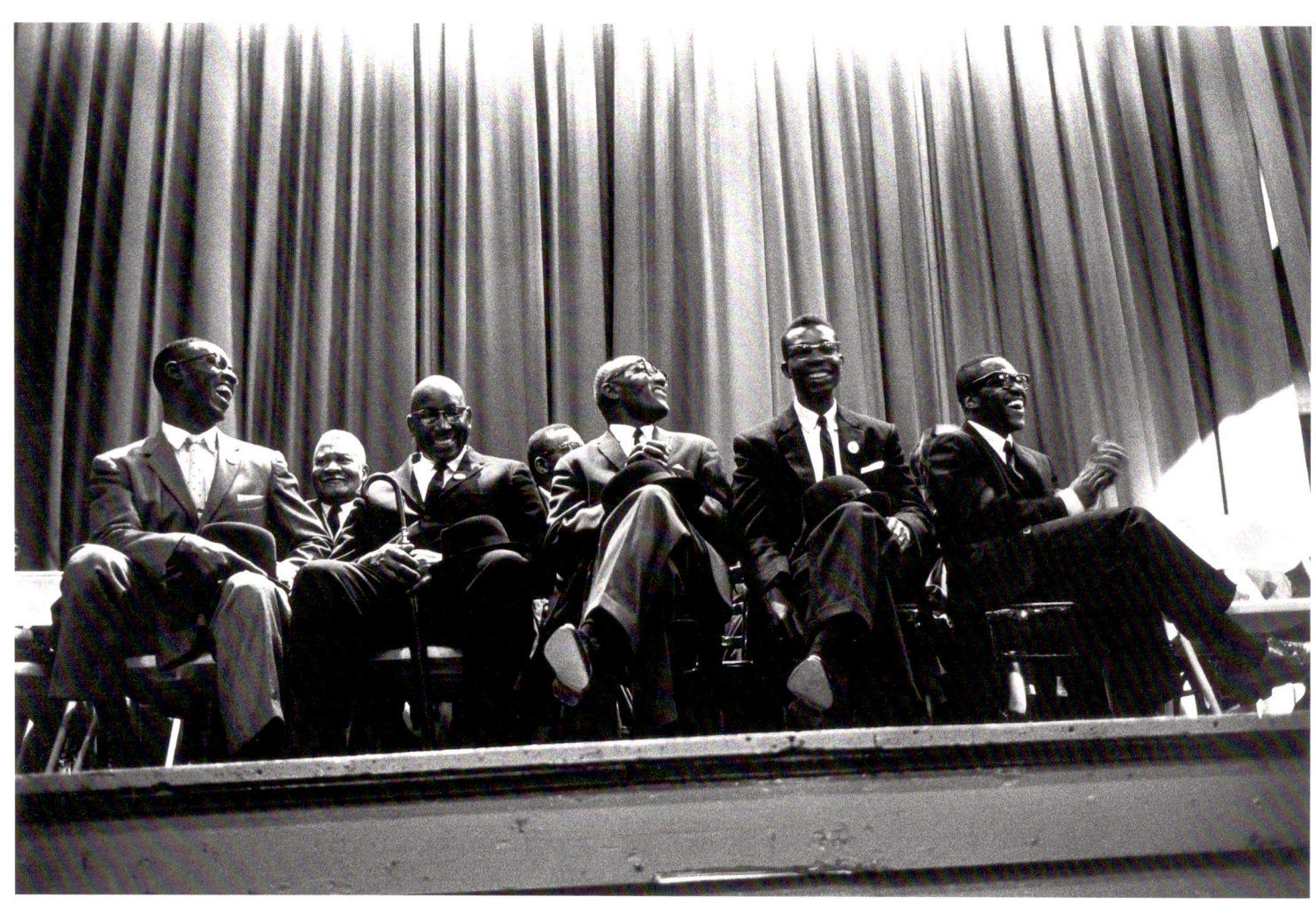

42. Dignitaries, Municipal Auditorium

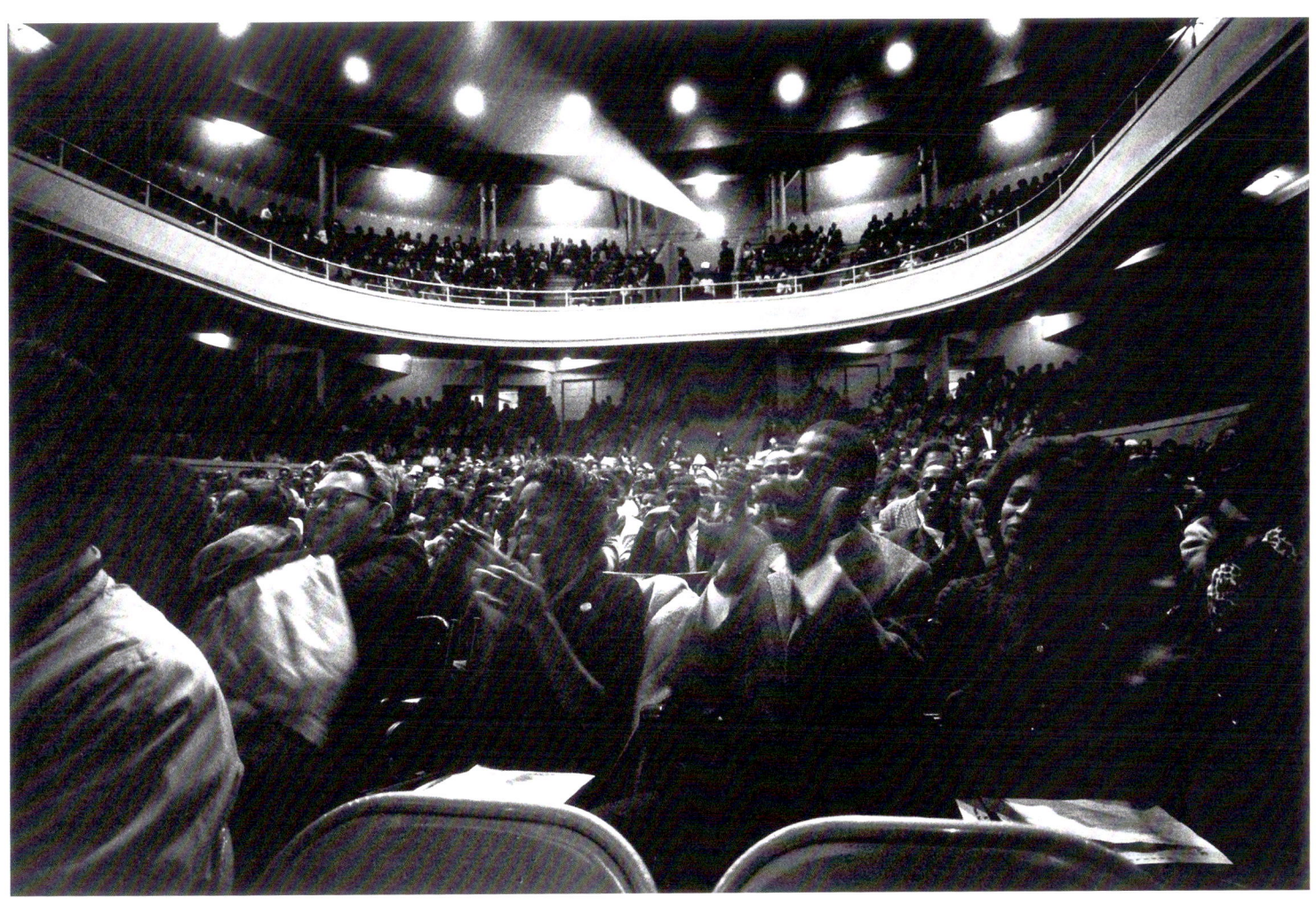

43. Dr. King Arrives, Municipal Auditorium

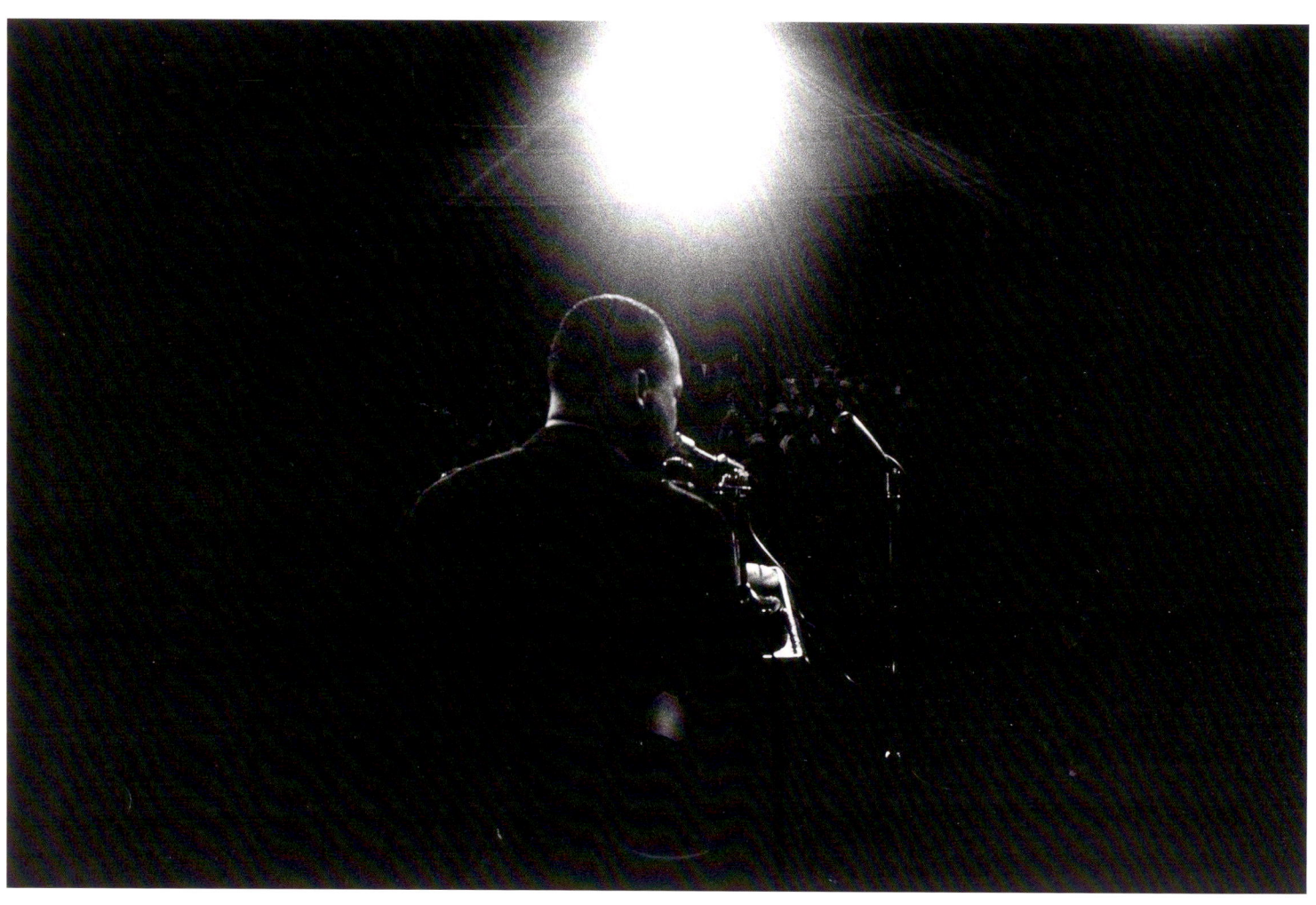

44. **Surveying the Audience,** Municipal Auditorium

I was there. It was a great meeting. We had never seen him in person before and he came at the request of the clergy, the black clergy, and he was a smooth talking, very knowledgeable guy about the movement. And he had an evangelistic candor, or close to the thing. And he had all the language we loved but had never heard any black speaker use in person. You can't imagine how this gets you, you know, and he came and told us that we were all going to be free. He promised us that if we worked at it we were going to make it. That was his, one of his great themes.

—Curtis Cooper

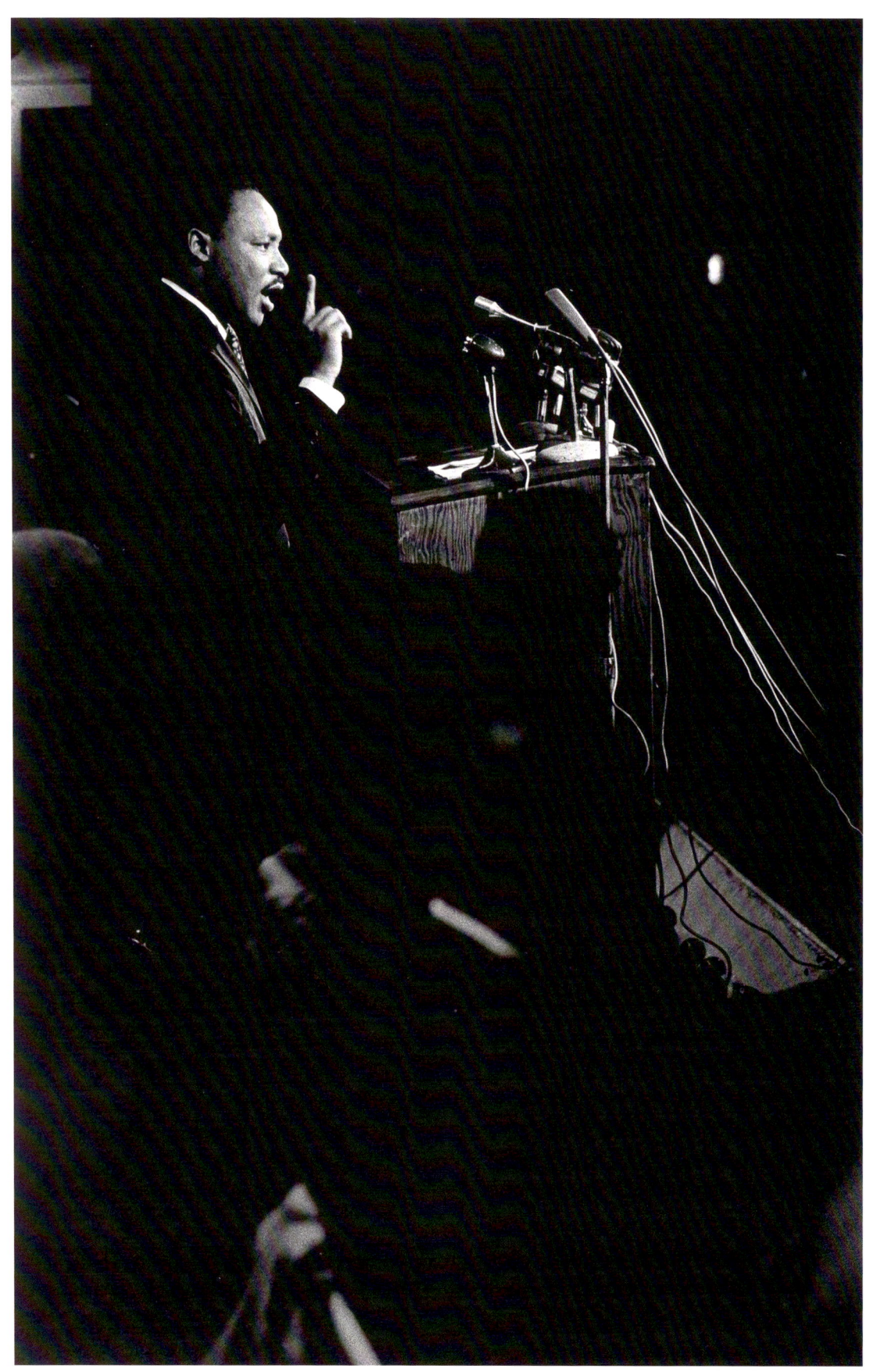

45. Emphasizing a Point, Municipal Auditorium

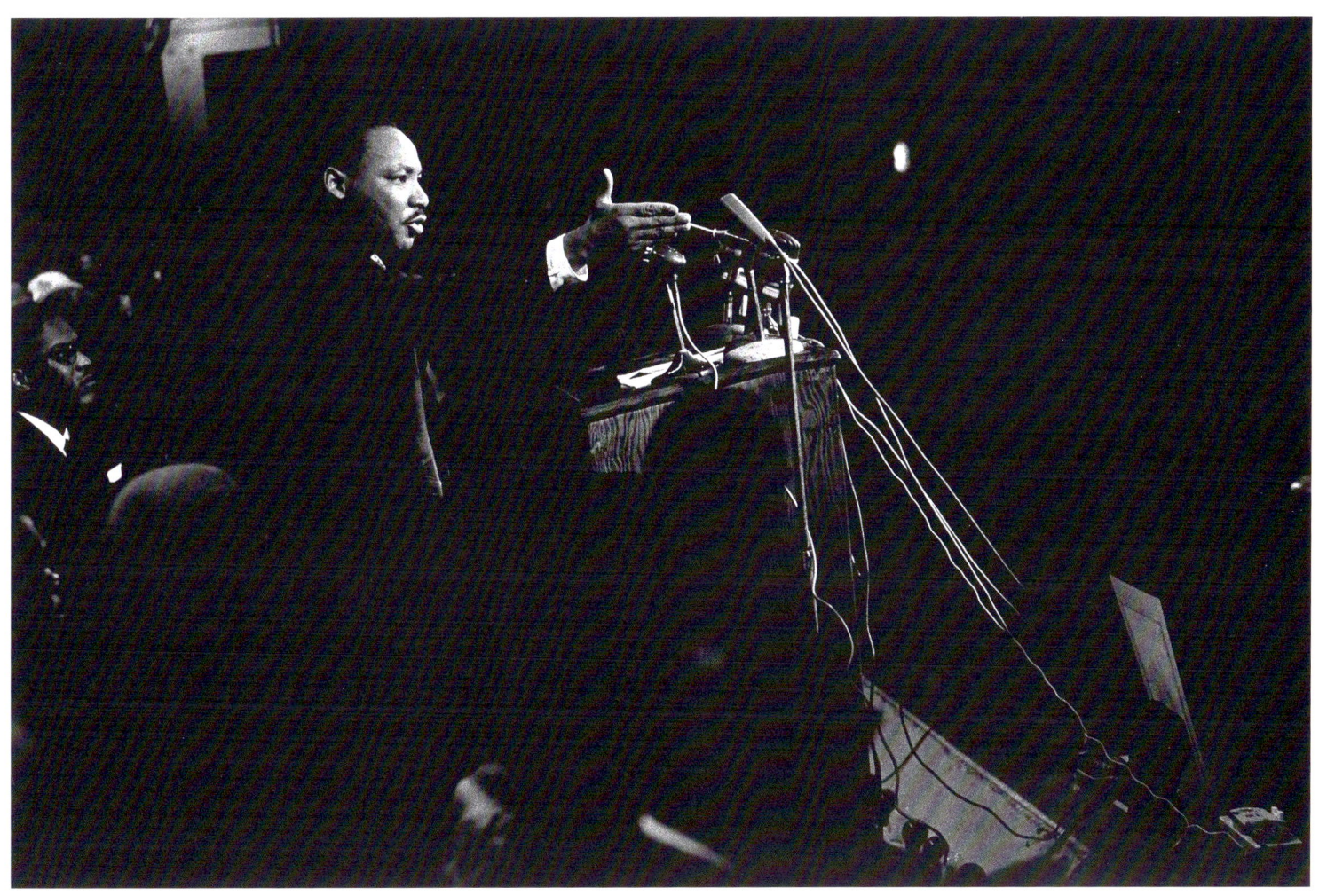

46. Reaching Out, Municipal Auditorium

The thing I remember about the speech (King gave in Savannah in 1964) was that—I often tell that story—he was preaching. I was, I'm a great observer of the crowd. I watch the crowd to try to read the crowd, see where they coming from and so forth. And I remember that night when Dr. King was speaking and…this guy was jumping up and down. I will never forget this, this guy was just jumping all up and down, "Yeah, Yeah, Yeah, Yeah."…And I asked this guy, "What did Dr. King say?" and, he said, " I don't know man, but it damned sure sounded good to me." Dr. King really talked mainly about the reality that we had proven it could happen and 'cause it hadn't happened no place else. They had not integrated the city, you know, so he was talking about it could happen.

—Hosea L. Williams

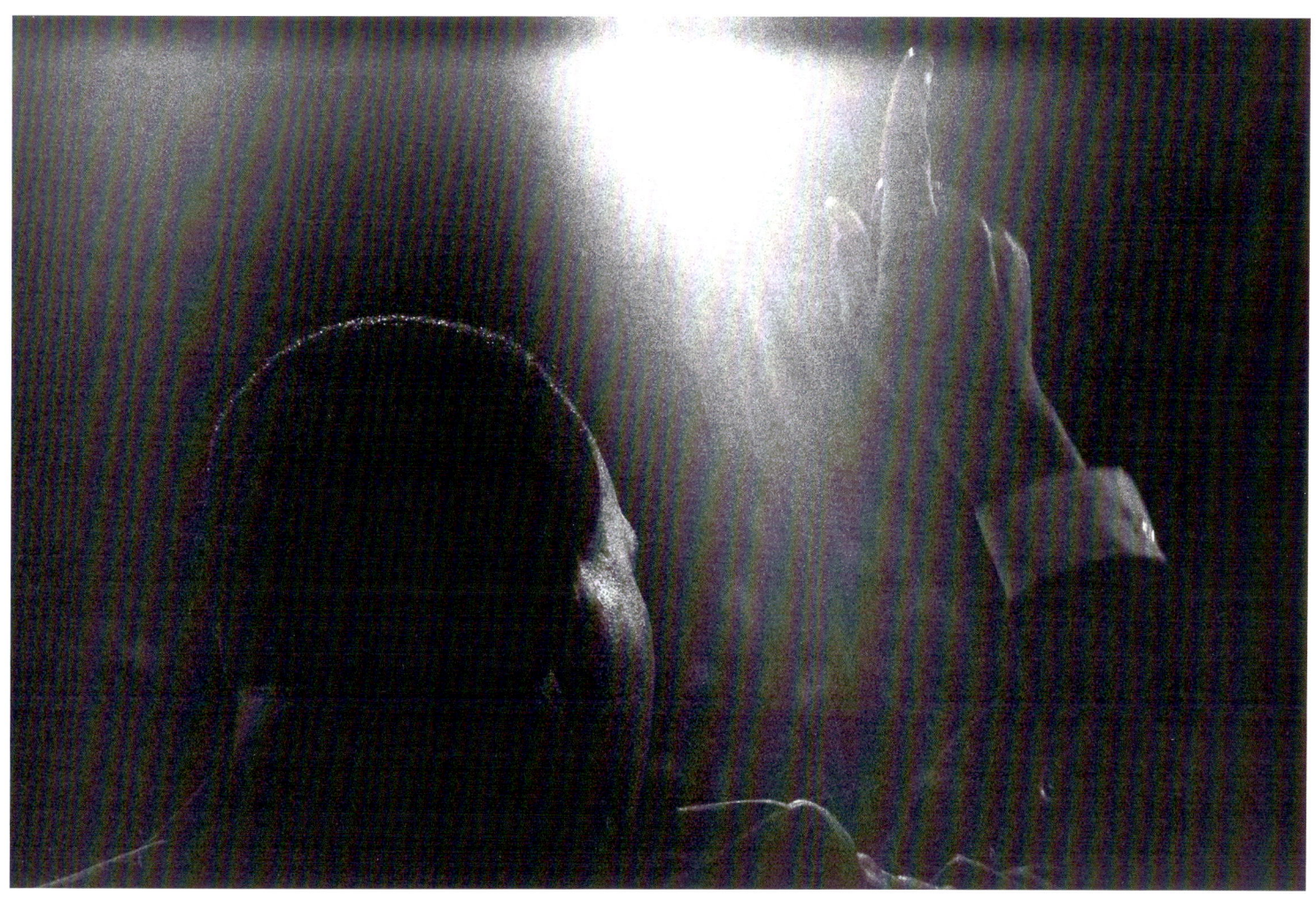

47. Inspiration, Municipal Auditorium

Image Plate Checklist

Freedom's March

Photographs of the Civil Rights Movement in Savannah by Frederick C. Baldwin

All images copyrighted by the artist unless otherwise indicated.

Frederick C. Baldwin
(American, b. 1929)
Long-term loan from the artist to the Telfair Museum of Art.

1. *"Big Lester" Among the Longshoremen, Longshoremen's Hall*, 1964
   Gelatin silver print
   9 ⅛ x 13 ¹³⁄₁₆ inches

2. *Bystanders, Wright Square*, 1963
   Gelatin silver print
   13 ⅞ x 10 inches

3. *Hosea Williams, Longshoremen's Hall*, 1963
   Gelatin silver print
   9 ¹⁄₁₆ x 13 ⅞ inches

4. *The Registrar, Chatham County Courthouse*, 1963
   Gelatin silver print
   13 ¹⁵⁄₁₆ x 9 ³⁄₁₆ inches

5. *High School Students Waiting to Register, Chatham County Courthouse*, 1963
   Gelatin silver print
   9 ¹⁄₁₆ x 13 ⅞ inches

6. *"Big Lester" and "Trash" Recruiting Longshoremen, Longshoremen's Hall*, 1963
   Gelatin silver print
   9 ⅛ x 13 ⅞ inches

7. *"Trash" with Longshoremen, Longshoremen's Hall*, 1963
   Gelatin silver print
   13 ¹¹⁄₁₆ x 9 ¹⁄₁₆ inches

8. *Hosea Williams Preaching Voter Registration, Longshoremen's Hall*, 1963
   Gelatin silver print
   13 ⅞ x 9 inches

9. *Hosea Williams Discusses Voter Registration, Longshoremen's Hall*, 1963
   Gelatin silver print
   9 ⅛ x 13 ⅞ inches

10. *Skepticism, West Broad Street*, 1963
    Gelatin silver print
    9 ¹⁄₁₆ x 13 ⅞ inches

11. *Persistence, West Broad Street*, 1963
    Gelatin silver print
    9 ¹⁄₁₆ x 13 ¹³⁄₁₆ inches

12. *Success, West Broad Street*, 1963
    Gelatin silver print
    9 ¹⁄₁₆ x 13 ⅞ inches

13. *"Big Lester" Makes a Point*, 1963
    Gelatin silver print
    13 ⅞ x 9 ¹⁄₁₆ inches

14. *"Big Lester" Captivates*, 1964
    Gelatin silver print
    9 ⅛ x 13 ⅞ inches

15. *"Big Lester" Persuades the Patrons, West Broad Street*, 1963
    Gelatin silver print
    9 ¹⁄₁₆ x 13 ¾ inches

16. *No One Escapes Lester, West Broad Street*, 1963
    Gelatin silver print
    9 ¹⁄₁₆ x 13 ⅞ inches

17. *The Ballot Bus*, 1963
    Gelatin silver print
    9 ⅛ x 13 ¹³⁄₁₆ inches

18. *Counting Contributions*, 1963
    Gelatin silver print
    9 ⅛ x 13 ⅞ inches

19. *Civil Rights Workers Posing with Ballot Bus*, 1963
    Gelatin silver print
    9 ⅛ x 13 ⅞ inches

20. *Benjamin Van Clark Leading a March, Bull Street*, 1963
    Gelatin silver print
    13 ¹⁵⁄₁₆ x 9 ⅛ inches

21. *Freedom or Death*, 1963
    Gelatin silver print
    8 ¹³⁄₁₆ x 13 ¹³⁄₁₆ inches

22. *Voter Registration, Chatham County Courthouse*, 1963
    Gelatin silver print
    8 ¹⁵⁄₁₆ x 13 ⅞ inches

23. *Taking a Drag, Wright Square*, 1963
    Gelatin silver print
    9 ⅛ x 13 ⅞ inches

24. *Listening, Wright Square*, 1963
    Gelatin silver print
    13 ¹³⁄₁₆ x 9 ⅛ inches

25. *The Riot Squad*, 1963
    Gelatin silver print
    9 ⅛ x 13 ⅞ inches

26. *Hosea Williams Preaching from Tomo-Chi-Chi's Rock, Wright Square*, 1963
    Gelatin silver print
    9 ¹⁄₁₆ x 13 ¹³⁄₁₆ inches

27. *Singing Freedom Songs*, 1963
    Gelatin silver print
    13 ¾ x 8 ⅞ inches

28. *Marching for Freedom*, 1963
    Gelatin silver print
    9 ⅛ x 13 ⅞ inches

29. *Prayer, Wright Square*, 1963
    Gelatin silver print
    13 ¹⁵⁄₁₆ x 9 ¹⁄₁₆ inches

30. *Onlooker, Wright Square*, 1963
    Gelatin silver print
    13 ⅞ x 9 ⅛ inches

31. *Father and Child, Wright Square*, 1963
    Gelatin silver print
    13 ¹³⁄₁₆ x 9 inches

32. *Thinking*, 1963
    Gelatin silver print
    13 ⅞ x 9 ¹⁄₁₆ inches

33. *Audience, First African Baptist Church*, 1964
    Gelatin silver print
    8 ¹⁵⁄₁₆ x 13 ¾ inches

34. *Anticipation, First African Baptist Church*, 1964
    Gelatin silver print
    9 ⅛ x 13 ⅞ inches

35. *Waving Certificates of Courage, First African Baptist Church Basement,* 1964
    Gelatin silver print
    9 x 13 13/16 inches

36. *Mrs. King, First African Baptist Church,* 1964
    Gelatin silver print
    9 x 13 11/16 inches

37. *Andrew Young, Hosea Williams and B. Clarence Mayfield Waiting for Dr. King, Municipal Auditorium,* 1964
    Gelatin silver print
    9 1/8 x 13 7/8 inches

38. *Unpacking Handbills,* 1964
    Gelatin silver print
    13 15/16 x 9 inches

39. *Press Conference, Municipal Auditorium,* 1964
    Gelatin silver print
    13 7/8 x 9 1/8 inches

40. *A Moment of Relaxation, Municipal Auditorium,* 1963
    Gelatin silver print
    9 1/8 x 13 7/8 inches

41. *Sharing a Joke with the Press, Municipal Auditorium,* 1964
    Gelatin silver print
    13 7/8 x 9 1/8 inches

42. *Dignitaries, Municipal Auditorium,* 1964
    Gelatin silver print
    9 13/16 x 13 7/8 inches

43. *Dr. King Arrives, Municipal Auditorium,* 1964
    Gelatin silver print
    9 1/8 x 13 7/8 inches

44. *Surveying the Audience, Municipal Auditorium,* 1964
    Gelatin silver print
    9 1/8 x 13 7/8 inches

45. *Emphasizing a Point, Municipal Auditorium,* 1964
    Gelatin silver print
    13 7/8 x 9 inches

46. *Reaching Out, Municipal Auditorium,* 1964
    Gelatin silver print
    9 1/8 x 13 7/8 inches

47. *Inspiration, Municipal Auditorium,* 1964
    Gelatin silver print
    9 1/8 x 13 15/16 inches